H

THE WAR CHRONICLES

THE WAR

Action stories of
U.S. soldiers, sailors,
marines and airmen
in World War II

By DON HORAN

A LOU REDA BOOK

RICHARDSON & STEIRMAN, INC.
New York • 1988

CHRONICLES

Copyright © 1988 Don Horan

ISBN: 0-931933-60-9

Library of Congress Catalog Number: 87-061150

The publisher wishes to thank Mort Zimmerman for his brilliant work above and beyond the call of picture editing. The stunning results of his genius are seen throughout *The War Chronicles*.

10 9 8 7 6 5 4 3 2 1

CONTENTS

CHAPTER 1 THE ATTACK ON PEARL HARBOR

"Oahu is under attack. This is no joke!"

—Honolulu Radio 7:02 A.M. December 7, 1941.

In the early hours of November 25, 1941, while peace negotiations between the United States and Japan were being vigorously pursued in Washington, a Japanese task force moved out of Hikotappu Bay in the southern Kuriles and set course for Hawaii.

Vice Admiral Chuichi Nagumo had carefully plotted a circuitous route, one that would take his fleet through stormy, fogbound waters well north of the normal sea lanes. Strict radio silence was observed. Ahead of the 28-ship force, a squadron of Japanese submarines prowled restlessly, under orders to sink any ship encountered en route.

In the flagship wardroom, Nagumo and his fleet commanders huddled over maps of their assigned target, the American naval base at Pearl Harbor. The admiral's orders were clear: If the Washington negotiations proved successful, he was to return to base. If the talks broke off, a brief coded message from Tokyo would authorize the attack.

As the ships steamed through rising seas, flight crews tightened the deck lashings of the planes while ordnance personnel readied special-finned, shallow-water torpedoes and armor-piercing bombs.

In his radio room, the fleet's communications officer tensely monitored hourly reports of the ongoing negotiations in Washington.

Hours later, as a mighty east wind churned the sea into fury, Adm. Nagumo sat quietly in his cabin, wondering perhaps why destiny had chosen him to lead this historic mission, and if he would receive Tokyo's three-word order to bomb Pearl Harbor.

The United States and Japan had been on a collision course toward war for more than a decade. It began with Japan's occupation of Manchuria in 1931 and her invasion of the Chinese mainland six years later—events that provoked strong protests from Washington.

With world attention soon focused on Adolf Hitler's European conquests, Japan had seized the opportunity to further expand her influence in the Pacific.

While gravely aware of these threats from both the east and the west, Franklin Roosevelt's ability to act was gravely hampered. In the more than 20 years since World War I, America's geographical isolation had gradually fostered a spiritual isolation. The outbreak of hostilities in 1939 had given rise to a great national debate over what role the United States should play in the new conflict. Safe and secure behind their ocean ramparts, most Americans argued that what was happening in Europe and the Far East was a tragic but distant affair. It was, they felt, none of their concern.

Japan's signing of a 1940 Tripartite Pact with Hitler and Mussolini, however, seemed to give her a clear path for still further aggressive expansion. With the growing danger of a two-ocean confrontation, American isolationism began to erode. The average U.S. citizen was suddenly prepared to support a strong national defense. Roosevelt gained quick Congressional approval of his budget requests; compulsive military service was adopted. Lend Lease to Britain, standing alone against Hitler's madness, was dramatically increased. The United States had joined the fight—the self-proclaimed "arsenal of democracy."

But was America ready for war?

For years U.S. Pacific defenses had been the subject of much criticism. In a 1938 report, Admiral Thomas Hepburn, finding them "grossly inadequate," had urged an immediate expansion of Hawaii's naval and air facilities. Yet nothing was done to act on his recommendations.

Then, early in 1941, even as Adm. Yamamoto and the Japanese Imperial Staff discussed plans for a carrier attack on Hawaii, America's ambassador in Tokyo was warning of such a possibility. But Washington continued to insist that Malaya or the Philippines would be the likely targets of a Japanese move. Pearl Harbor, bulwark of America's Pacific defenses, remained on a peacetime footing.

It was Japan's brazen occupation of southern Indochina in July that finally forced Roosevelt's hand. With new land and air bases now within striking distance of the Philippines and Singapore, the Japanese posed a grave threat to British and U.S. Pacific interests. The president's response was immediate.

On July 25th Roosevelt froze all Japanese assets in the United States and imposed other strong economic sanctions. General Douglas MacArthur was named to command American forces in the Far East. The entire Pacific area was placed on alert.

With the unacceptable loss of vital oil supplies caused by the American embargo, Japan sought a way out. Her ambassador in Washington, Adm. Kishisaburo Nomura, proposed immediate talks aimed at solving U.S.-Japanese differences. Nomura, a six-foot Annapolis graduate, was staunchly pro-American. But time was running out. In August, with his country hurtling toward war with America, Nomura began the delicate negotiations in Washington.

Adm. Nagumo's flagship plowed through heavy seas. From the bridge, he watched as air crews gathered on the flight deck for yet another in an endless series of combat briefings. Small groups gathered about aerial photographs and charts of Pearl Harbor. Flight commanders faced them, repeating to each other the attack plan over and over.

Turbulent weather and boiling seas had plagued Nagumo's journey. But his devious route had been wisely chosen. During the force's week at sea, no other ship had been seen.

On the previous day, his communications center had intercepted the coded message—EAST WINDS, RAIN—an order to all Japanese diplomatic offices to begin the destruction of sensitive papers. Despite the continuing peace talks in Washington, Nagumo knew that war was very close.

In his carrier quarters, Capt. Mitsuo Fuchida, chosen to lead the aerial strike on Pearl Harbor, studied the latest intelligence briefings from Japanese agents in Hawaii. They indicated that all eight of the Pacific Fleet's battleships would be in port by the weekend. The planes based at nearby Hickam and Wheeler fields remained tightly grouped as a protection against sabotage. This pleased Fuchida. They would make inviting targets for his pilots.

The heavy roll of the ship frightened him. Fuchida knew that the fleet was scheduled to refuel on the following morning. He prayed that the seas would calm in time.

On the bridge, Adm. Nagumo was handed the latest wireless report on the peace talks. The final American offer had been dispatched to Tokyo and was being reviewed. The report referred to it as "an ultimatum." Nagumo could read between the lines. He was certain now of what lay ahead.

The talks in Washington had not gone well. For all his good intentions, Ambassador Nomura had turned out to be a vacillating, frequently ambiguous negotiator whose diplomatic inexperience soon became apparent.

For this reason, Lt. Gen. Hideki Tojo, Japan's extremist Prime Minister, had dispatched politically wise Saburo Kurusu as a Special Ambassador to assist Nomura. While privately conceding that war with America was inevitable, Tojo knew that the diplomatic game had to be played out.

On November 15th, in an atmosphere of politeness and protocol, Kurusu arrived in Washington to begin last-ditch discussions with American Secretary of State Cordell Hull. The pace of the negotiations quickened immediately. On the 17th, Kurusu presented a list of "minimal demands." They asked for an immediate end to the American economic embargo, cessation of all U.S. military and economic aid to China, and acknowledgment of Japan's Greater East Asia Co-Prosperity Sphere. Kurusu urged that the note be passed to Roosevelt and Hull without delay. Time, he cautioned, was running out.

On November 26th, Nomura and Kurusu were summoned to the State Department and handed America's strongly worded reply. It demanded, among other things, Japan's immediate withdrawal from China and Indo-China and her recognition of Chiang Kai shek's Chinese government. It also called for an end to Japan's involvement with the Axis nations. Kurusu and Nomura, visibly upset by the tone of the note, left the State Department promptly and without comment.

On the following morning, in his Pearl Harbor office, Adm. Husband Kimmel, Commander in Chief of the Pacific Fleet, was handed an important communication from Washington. "This dispatch is to be considered a war warning," it began, and went on to tell Kimmel to expect an aggressive move by the Japanese within days. It suggested that the Philippines or Malaya would be the likely targets, but made no mention of a possible attack against Pearl Harbor.

December 1st. At an Imperial Conference in Tokyo attended by Emperor Hirohito, Prime Minister Tojo and the Japanese General Staff made the irrevocable decision for war against America. Pearl Harbor would be attacked at 8:00 A.M., December 7th, Hawaiian time.

The following morning, after a dangerous refueling in high seas, Adm. Nagumo received the three-word message CLIMB MOUNT NIKITA. He sat alone for several minutes, solemnly considering his sacred mission. Then, summoning his deputy, he ordered a meeting of all task force commanders within the hour.

In Washington, Gen. George C. Marshall, Army Chief of Staff, realizing that the peace talks had broken down, sent an urgent message to Gen. Walter C. Short, Army Commander at Pearl Harbor. It ordered Short to place all troops under his command on full alert. But due to an incredible series of communications blunders, the message arrived too late.

December 7th. Kurusu and Nomura, having received their government's coded reply to the American demands, called to request a 1:00 P.M. meeting with the Secretary of State. Cordell Hull agreed to see them at 1:45. Then, as the two envoys watched, members of the Japanese embassy staff began decoding the long message from Tokyo.

Just before dawn, 275 miles north of Oahu, as Adm. Nagumo's carriers turned slowly into the wind, Capt. Mitsuo Fuchida issued his final instructions to the Pearl Harbor strike force. Then, after praying briefly before a Shinto shrine, he climbed to the windswept flight deck.

Shortly after 6 A.M., Fuchida taxied into position. With the carrier's battle flags snapping in the stiff wind and Japanese sailors cheering wildly, his plane roared down the flight deck and gently rose into the dawn sky. Some 359 others on six carriers would shortly follow.

At Pearl, the huge antitorpedo gates, guarding the harbor's 2,500-foot entrance, slowly cranked open, a usual morning procedure. Several miles away, seven battleships of the Pacific fleet were anchored along one side of Ford Island. Hardly a hundred feet separated one from the other. An eighth, the U.S.S. *Pennsylvania*, was in a nearby drydock, undergoing repairs.

At the radar station on Kahuku Point, Pvt. Joseph L. Lockhard, the operator, yawned wearily. Along with Pvt. George E. Elliott, the plotter, Lockhard was working the widely unpopular 4–7 A.M. shift, instituted following the recent "war warning" alert. To make matters worse, Elliott had asked for an extra hour's training on the oscilloscope at the end of their shift. Lockhard had reluctantly agreed.

Capt. Fuchida's planes raced for Pearl, the ocean below them obscured by a dense layer of clouds. Fuchida worried about his course. Strong headwinds had almost certainly affected his path of flight. Nervously, he twisted the radio dial until a clear signal from the Honolulu station came through. Checked against the radio direction finder, it showed his first-wave strike force was five degrees off course. Fuchida made the correction, then settled back. Pearl Harbor was 30 minutes away.

At Kahuku Point, Pvt. Lockhard watched as George Elliott made another adjustment on the oscilloscope's controls. It was a little after 7 A.M. and Lockhard had decided he'd call a halt to the training session no later than 7:30. Elliott signaled with his hand, indicating a cluster of targets to the north. Lockhard beckoned him aside and checked the scope.

Several minutes later, having plotted the movement of many planes 137 miles to the north, Lockhard called the base Information Center. Lt. Kermit Tyler, an inexperienced Air Corps officer waiting to be relieved, listened to Lockhard's report. Tyler knew that a flight of B-17s from the mainland was expected momentarily. He told Lockhard the radar contact was "nothing to worry about." Satisfied, Lockhard hung up the phone and watched as Elliott continued to practice plot the approaching planes.

Saburo Kurusu fussed at the embassy workers decoding the Tokyo message. It was taking longer than anticipated and he worried that he and Nomura would be late for their meeting with Cordell Hull.

7:50 A.M. As the leaden clouds over Pearl Harbor suddenly parted and the morning sun appeared, Capt. Fuchida's 189-plane strike force swept in over Diamond Head. The lead group of bombers and fighters struck immediately at Hickam and Wheeler fields, bombing and strafing the aircraft parked wingtip to wingtip. Stunned defenders yanked machine guns from burning planes and returned the fire. Automobiles were driven onto the runways to prevent the possibility of troop landings. Small groups of pilots managed to get their planes airborne where they attacked the vastly superior Japanese forces. The first of Fuchida's warriors spun earthward.

On board the battleships lined up at Ford Island, sailors watched in horror as torpedo and dive bombers swooped down out of the blazing sun. The *Arizona* took a direct hit in her forward magazine and exploded with a horrendous roar. Others of the 94 ships anchored—cruisers, destroyers, and auxiliary craft—also fell victim to the rampaging planes. Pearl Harbor was quickly shrouded in a pall of black smoke. Wounded men stumbled about. Dead bodies littered the scene.

Blazing furiously, the battleship *Oklahoma* capsized at her berth. The *Nevada* managed to get underway but was later beached at Waipio Point. Every one of the other battleships was badly damaged. Long before the first wave flew off to the northwest, it was clear that America had suffered a terrible tragedy.

Forty-five minutes after the first assault, a second wave of 171 Japanese planes swept in over Pearl. On battleship row, the already devastated dreadnoughts were struck again and again. Several smaller craft were torpedoed by midget submarines that had infiltrated the harbor through the open net. New attacks were launched against the hangars and open fields of the air stations. A canopy of black smoke hung over America's premier naval base. In less than two hours, the U.S. Pacific fleet had been dealt a crippling blow.

At 2:05 P.M. Washington time, twenty minutes late, Saburo Kurusu and Adm. Nomura arrived at the State Department for their meeting with Cordell Hull. They were asked to wait.

Fifteen minutes later, a livid Hull, having learned of the Japanese treachery, summoned them to his office.

As suddenly as it began, the Japanese attack ended. Mitsuo Fuchida's second wave flew off to the north, leaving the port in ruins. All of the fleet's eight battleships were either sunk or listing badly; 347 of 394 planes had been destroyed. Casualties, civilian and military, numbered in the thousands. Delivery vans were stripped to serve as makeshift ambulances. People lined up at area hospitals to donate blood. Panic-stricken wives searched for husbands, parents for their children. Everywhere there was death and destruction.

In just 110 terror-filled minutes, the Japanese had gained mastery of the Pacific. Yet there was something to be thankful for. Pearl Harbor's oil storage areas had not been hit. The port's repair facilities remained untouched. They would be put to good use rebuilding the devastated fleet. Within two years, every battleship except the *Arizona* would be returned to active duty.

Three fleet carriers, the *Lexington, Saratoga,* and *Enterprise,* had been spared. Due to arrive at Pearl before the attack, they had been delayed at sea by extended maneuvers. Now, along with 20 cruisers and 65 destroyers, they represented America's entire strike force in the Pacific. Within six months, joined by the *Hornet* and *Yorktown* from the Atlantic, they would inflict a crippling defeat on the Japanese navy at Midway, one that would turn the tide of the Pacific war.

Throughout the United States, the sneak attack at Pearl Harbor gave rise to a great wave of indignation and outrage. Coupled with a sense of mortal danger, it united America as never before.

But 2,403 Americans were already dead, the nation's first victims of the great conflict that lay ahead. Of these, 1,106 were forever entombed in the shattered hull of the U.S.S. *Arizona.* Her superstructure, rising above the placid waters of Pearl Harbor, would remain a tragic reminder of a fateful day when America went to war.

Pearl Harbor on December 7, 1941. The fuel depot in flames after being strafed by planes from a Japanese aircraft carrier.

Smoke from Hickam Field and Pearl Harbor. This photograph was taken on the highway near the John Rodgers Airport Road on December 7, 1941.

The new Hickam Barracks in flames after strafing by Japanese aircraft. The photograph was taken on December 7, 1941.

Pearl Harbor, December 7, 1941. Bomb craters after the Japanese bombing of Hickam Field.

Bellows Field, Pearl Harbor. A flight of B-17's was caught in the attack on Pearl Harbor. This B-17 made a forced landing.

An LST disintegrates in a terrific explosion. A fireboat lies close by. West Loch, Pearl Harbor.

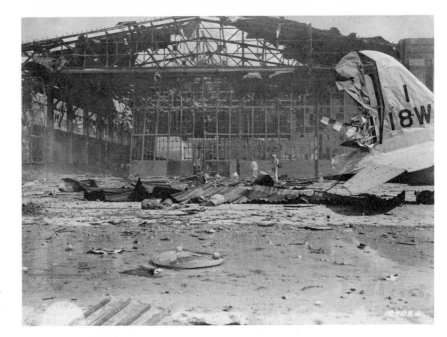

Pearl Harbor. Hangar No. 11 is a shell after strafing by Japanese bombers on December 7, 1941.

Fireboats close in on LST's struck during the Japanese attack. This photograph was taken on December 7, 1941, at West Loch.

The battleships *West Virginia* and *Tennessee* burn during the Pearl Harbor attack. Both ships made their way back to West Coast shipyards three weeks later to undergo extensive repairs.

The battleship *Arizona* was repeatedly hit by Japanese torpedo planes. Here she is under heavy attack. The photograph was taken during the heaviest Japanese attack.

December 7, 1941. A photograph taken from the bridge of one of Vice Admiral Chuichi Nagumo's Strike Force aircraft carriers. 51 bombers, 89 torpedo planes, and 43 fighters took off in the first wave. The second wave was of equal size.

Hickam Field became an inferno, repeatedly struck by Japanese bombs. The attacks wiped out all the U.S. air power stationed at Pearl Harbor.

A view of the Mole on December 7, 1941. Flames rise from damage inflicted by Japanese torpedo aircraft. A total of 361 planes attacked in two waves.

The battleship *Arizona* was repeatedly hit by Japanese torpedo planes and bombers on December 7th. She slowly turned over and settled on the bottom. Most of the crew is still entombed in her hull. The *Arizona* is now a national monument visited by thousands of people each month.

Bellows Field, Pearl Harbor, December 7, 1941. A gasoline truck caught in the open was strafed by a Japanese fighter and set afire. It then exploded. The photograph was taken after the first-wave attack.

THE WAR IN EUROPE

2 THE INVASION OF NORTH AFRICA

"An operation undertaken in an atmosphere of unrelieved improvisation and haste."

—Official army historian on Operation Torch.

At dusk on October 22, 1942, several miles off the mist-shrouded coast of Algeria, the British submarine *Seraph* gracefully rose to the Mediterranean surface.

Moments later, a knot of military officers appeared on deck. They scanned the distant North African shoreline through high-powered binoculars, watching as lights in the seaside village of Cherchell blinked on.

The men were interested in one light only—a lamp burning in the seaward window of a lonely farmhouse. It told them that those who had brought them on their perilous mission were waiting ashore.

Among the officers aboard the *Seraph* Maj. Gen. Mark W. Clark, deputy to European Commander Dwight Eisenhower. Clark, a lanky fearless soldier, was anxious to get ashore. There were urgent matters to be discussed and time was desperately short.

While a team of commandoes stood by, rubber boats at the ready, Clark was advised that the seas were too high for a landing attempt. The general protested sharply, but the submarine captain would not be moved. Their mission, he said, would have to be postponed for 24 hours.

The deck was cleared. Moments later, the *Seraph* again submerged beneath the choppy waters of the Mediterranean. The military decision that prompted Clark's journey to North Africa had been taken months before at Washington meetings between Franklin Roosevelt and Winston Churchill.

Determined to regain control of the Mediterranean, the British prime minister vigorously pressed for landings in North Africa, close to the desert fighting that had gone on for two years. With Field Marshal Erwin Rommel again on the offensive, Churchill sought to provide relief for his beleaguered desert army while securing a Mediterranean base for future operations against Sicily and Italy.

Roosevelt listened sympathetically, eager to placate the Russians, who had long demanded an Allied second front.

On July 25, 1942, the two Allied leaders had signed an agreement providing for Operation Torch—Anglo-American landings on the coast of northwest Africa. They were targeted for early November.

Planning began in earnest. Widespread Allied forces were earmarked for special training. U.S. and British officers met to meld their diverse military procedures into one seamless effort.

Conflicting national interests soon emerged.

The British insisted on landings inside the Mediterranean, on the coast of Algeria, to be followed by a quick dash for Tunisia before the Germans were able to reinforce that area.

Concerned with roving Mediterranean U-boat packs and the close proximity of Axis aircraft based in Sicily and Italy, America favored landings on the Atlantic coast of North Africa.

After spirited, often vitriolic negotiations, an invasion plan acceptable to all was formulated:

Three separate task forces would carry out landings at as many locations. Those in Algeria, at Oran and Algiers, would take place inside the Mediterranean. A third, the principal American operation, would go ashore at Casablanca, on the Atlantic coast of Morocco.

Crucial questions existed as to the possible reaction of French military forces in North Africa. The rank and file of their army and navy was known to be largely sympathetic to the Allied cause. But many high-ranking officers were staunch supporters of the pro-Nazi Vichy government of Marshal Henri Petain. Since the 1940 armistice with Germany provided that the French must resist any Allied attempt to seize North Africa, it was feared they would strongly oppose the Torch landings.

As D-Day approached, it was imperative that the Allies gather information relative to French military strength and deployment in the Torch landing areas. Robert D. Murphy, President Roosevelt's special representative in North Africa, began contacting sympathetic French leaders, men who wished to avoid a bloodbath when the Allies landed. They suggested that a high-ranking American officer be sent to meet with them. Gen. Eisenhower personally selected Mark Clark to undertake the hazardous mission.

During the daylight hours of October 23rd, the submarine *Seraph* remained submerged. In his cramped quarters, waiting anxiously for sunset, Gen. Clark received regular reports on sea conditions at the surface.

On shore, at an upper window of the seaside farmhouse, Robert Murphy looked out at the placid Mediterranean, grateful that the seas had calmed. Nothing should prevent Clark and his party from landing that evening.

The whispered conversations of those waiting to meet the American general drifted up from below. Murphy had chosen the group carefully. Gen. Charles Mast led the military officers supporting the invasion. The Gaullist mayor of Algiers was also present. With sunset just minutes away, Murphy lit the bedroom signal lamp, then went below to join the others.

Forty minutes later, the *Seraph* gently rose from beneath the sea. Clark and his armed party emerged, took to their rubber boats and rowed into the deepening dusk.

During the course of an all-night meeting, Gen. Mast gave Clark the position and strength of all French units in the three landing areas. Other information vital to the success of the invasion was also exchanged.

With the landings just two weeks off, Clark knew he must get his facts into the hands of Allied planners. But evening again brought high seas and the group was unable to return to the submarine waiting offshore.

On the next night, after barely avoiding detection by local police, Clark and his party successfully launched their rubber boats and returned to the *Seraph*.

Hours later, in mid-Mediterranean, he was picked up by an Allied flying boat and taken to London. After reviewing Clark's information, the Torch invasion plan was hastily altered. Clark did not know that at 2140 hours on October 23rd, while he was holding his clandestine meeting on the Algerian coast, the crucial battle of El Alamein had erupted in the Egyptian desert.

For 10 days, Erwin Rommel's Afrika Korps struggled valiantly to contain the numerically superior forces of Bernard Montgomery's British VIII Army. But Rommel knew the situation was hopeless. By early November, despite Hitler's maniacal exhortations to hold the line, the German Field Marshal began a general withdrawal westward.

On November 7th, at his Gibraltar command post, Gen. Eisenhower held a top secret meeting with French Gen. Henri Giraud, a military hero and recent escapee from imprisonment in a German fortress.

Spirited to Gibraltar by submarine, Giraud was offered command of all French forces in North Africa following the landings. His presence on the Allied side, Eisenhower knew, would be of inestimable value. Surprisingly, Giraud refused the offer, insisting that he be placed in supreme command of the entire operation. After a stormy session, the French general reluctantly agreed to Eisenhower's terms.

Later that same evening, outside the Mediterranean, the 700 ships comprising Operation Torch's armada separated into three groups. While the Western Task Force under Maj. Gen. George Patton made for the Atlantic beaches around Casablanca, the Central and Eastern Task Forces sailed past Gibraltar and into the Mediterranean, bound, respectively, for Oran and Algiers.

In the predawn hours of November 8th, Patton's assault forces hit the Moroccan beaches.

At Mehdia, 65 miles to the north of Casablanca, elements of the U.S. 2nd Armored and 9th Infantry divisions raced ashore.

Fifty miles closer to the city, at Fedela, units of the U.S. 3rd Infantry Division established a beachhead after heavy fighting.

At Safi, 200 miles south of Casablanca, other elements of the 2nd Armored and 9th Infantry divisions battled inland.

The French resisted bitterly at all points.

At Mehdia, the American destroyer *Dallas* rammed a defense net and proceeded up the Sebou River to a point close to the airfield at Port Lyautey. The vital strip fell after several days of costly fighting.

At Fedela, gutsy American destroyers went in close to blast the shore batteries harassing the invasion fleet.

At Safi, two World War I destroyers, masts cut down to provide a low silhouette, dashed headlong into the harbor and landed their assault troops dockside.

By November 10th American forces north and south of Casablanca were advancing on the city.

In the Mediterranean, the combined British and American landings also met determined opposition by the French defenders.

At Oran the Center Task Force, including American units, landed at points east and west of that Algerian port. A suicide force aboard two Coast Guard cutters attempted to crash the city's harbor, but was driven off with heavy casualties.

At Algiers, the Eastern Task Force, mostly British, landed at three points. A force of 650 Americans, making a shipboard assault against the harbor, took several objectives before they were overwhelmed and captured by superior numbers.

By far the most dramatic development of the entire invasion occurred inside Algiers when French Admiral Jean François Darlan, deputy to Vichy leader Henri Petain, was captured while visiting his ailing son. Generals Clark and Giraud rushed there in an attempt to negotiate a cease-fire with the French official.

On November 11th, after much vacillation, Darlan agreed to a truce, ending hostilities in French North Africa.

The first phase of Operation Torch was over. The race for Tunis and Bizerte was on.

As Rommel's Afrika Korps continued its westward retreat from El Alamein, Torch forces of Gen. Kenneth Anderson's Anglo-American First Army began a headlong dash for the Tunisian border. In his determination to capture Tunis and Bizerte, 400 miles to the east, before the arrival of Axis reinforcements, Eisenhower urged Anderson to advance at full speed. At the same time, American and British forces at Casablanca and Oran raced eastward to join up with Anderson's understrength army.

But North Africa's terrain was inhospitable, its weather uncooperative. As the Germans took over Tunisia's airfields, Anderson's advance was subjected to heavy Luftwaffe attacks. All the while, Axis troops and materiel were pouring into Tunisia from Sicily and Italy.

On the morning of November 17th, a spearhead of Anderson's First Army ran headlong into a German battle group probing westward, the first contact between the opposing forces. The Germans were driven off and Anderson continued his advance.

To the south, an American tank unit known as Blade Force roared through the valley of the Medjerda River, toward Tunis.

With winter fast approaching, Anderson pressed his attacks. Inland, Blade Force tanks hammered at Medjez el Bab, 35 miles southwest of Tunis. Coast forces assaulted Mateur, the last important rail junction before Bizerte. When Djedeida fell, Allied troops were only 10 miles from Tunis.

But First Army supplies and equipment were well behind their advance units. Tanks attempting to reach the front foundered on the treacherous Tunisian roads. Anderson found it impossible to build up sufficient strength to mount a final attack against Tunis and Bizerte.

Then, the rains came in earnest.

On December 24th, with resistance stiffening all along the line, Eisenhower realized he had lost the race. Anderson was ordered to halt the 44-day offensive heartbreakingly short of his goal.

Winter closed in; the front fell into stalemate. The Allied conquest of North Africa was put on hold.

To the east, in the Libyan desert, Gen. Montgomery's VIII Army continued its westward pursuit of Erwin Rommel's battered Panzerarmee Afrika. Having bypassed Tobruk, British forces retook Benghazi. By mid-December, after a five-week, 700-mile advance, Montgomery stood before Marsa el Brega, a desert defensive position that had defied all previous VIII Army attempts at penetration.

But this time Rommel was not disposed to make a stand. With his desert army starved of reinforcements and supplies, he knew that a prolonged defense could only spell disaster. Disregarding Hitler's order to stand or die, he resumed his retreat at flank speed.

The dawning of 1943 saw the brief Tunisian stalemate suddenly end. German and Italian forces of Gen. Jurgin von Arnim's newly formed 5th Panzerarmee began attacks against French forces holding the crucial mountain passes of the eastern Dorsals. The reserve-short French fell back.

Buoyed by the victory, Von Arnim moved to exploit his gains. Before American counterattacks could stop his advance, the German commander held all the passes of the eastern Dorsals.

On January 23rd Rommel abandoned Tripoli. Three days later, his exhausted army ended a 1,500-mile retreat when they crossed into Tunisia and took up positions along the Mareth Line, a series of aging French fortifications.

Planning to attack Anderson before the arrival of the plodding Montgomery, Rommel joined forces with Von Arnim. Their combined army now numbered 160,000 picked troops. Rommel readied his attack.

During mid-January, Roosevelt and Churchill met at Casablanca to discuss Allied war aims for 1943. These included maintenance of the initiative and extension of the war to other theaters.

In a historic announcement following the conference, Roosevelt stated that the enemy would be battled until the Allies had achieved "unconditional surrender."

In mid-February 1943, as British VIII Army units began trickling into Tunisia, the German panzers struck Anderson's army.

Rommel's two-pronged attack in the south drove for Gafsa and the western Dorsal passes at Sbiba and Kasserine.

In the north, Von Arnim's columns smashed against the other mountain passes. Their fall would lay open the Tunisian hinterland and all of Algeria. The entire Allied campaign in North Africa hung in the balance.

Rommel raced for the Kasserine Pass, an ancient Tunisian battleground. Here, Carthaginians and Vandals, the legions of Caesar, and horsemen of old Arab civilizations had struggled.

On February 14th his panzers struck the weak, disorganized American II Corps holding the pass. With nothing to stop the awesome Tiger tanks with their 88mm cannons, the Americans fell back in dismay.

Flush with victory, Rommel and Von Arnim drove on with uncontrollable fury, occupying the key towns of Sidi bou Zid and Gafsa.

But the Americans, joined by British armor, regrouped and counterattacked. Newly arrived Grant and Sherman tanks joined the assault. The German advance, which had overrun more than 4,000 square miles of Tunisia, ground to a halt. Within a week, they withdrew through the mountain passes, ending the Axis threat.

On March 6th, in a final, desperate effort to turn the tide, Rommel sped southeast to launch a powerful armored attack against Montgomery's positions at Medenine, holding the southern end of the Mareth Line. But Allied intelligence learned of the plan and British artillery was waiting. Attacking into the face of 500 British antitank guns, Rommel's armor was torn to pieces.

Two days later, ill and disillusioned, the German Field Marshal flew to Berlin, where he argued that the campaign was hopelessly lost. He begged Hitler to evacuate the remaining German forces in North Africa. His pleas were in vain.

Meanwhile, George Patton, now commanding the U.S. II Corps, was spoiling for a fight. The pugnacious tank officer drove his armor eastward, storming into Gafsa on March 17th. Ten days later, his forces mauled the still powerful German 10th Panzer Division and captured El Guettar.

Having flanked the Mareth Line and broken through the Axis positions, Montgomery's VIII Army now joined up with Patton's II Corps. Forming a solid Allied front, the two armies set out in pursuit of the wildly retreating enemy.

Von Arnim, who had succeeded Rommel, was ordered to hold Tunisia at all costs. But his 16 shattered, outnumbered divisions were critically short of petrol and ammunition. The German commander had no choice but to retreat toward Tunis and Bizerte.

The final days of the campaign were at hand. While the U.S. II Corps, now led by Maj. Gen. Omar N. Bradley, attacked toward Bizerte, Kenneth Anderson's First Army advanced on Tunis. With Montgomery exerting pressure from the south, the Axis forces were driven into an ever-narrowing piece of northeast Tunisia.

On May 7th, led by the crack 11th Hussars, the British 7th Armored Division entered Tunis. At the same time, the U.S. 9th Division smashed into Bizerte. The surviving Axis troops vainly sought refuge on the Cape Bon peninsula.

On May 12th, the destruction of the German 90th Light Division at Bou Ficha signaled the end of hostilities in North Africa.

A quarter of a million German and Italian prisoners were taken, Gen. von Arnim among them. Erwin Rommel's once-feared Afrika Korps had ceased to exist. Only 638 Axis soldiers succeeded in reaching the safety of Italy.

From the still-smoldering shores of Tunisia, the Allied conquerors looked hungrily northward. Sicily, Italy, and southern France now lay open to invasion. It had been a glorious victory.

French Morocco. The beach at Fedsia on November 8, 1942, after successful landing of American troops. The beach is littered with discarded lifebelts.

The 1st Division landing at Andalouses, Algeria, on November 8, 1942. A road grader is being brought ashore. It will be used for clearing roads.

The 105th C.A. (AA) Battery C in Andalouses, Algeria. Soldiers are dug in, occupying a forward defense line near the beach.
November 10, 1942.

Near Oran, Algeria, November 10, 1942.
American GI's in the field. The soldier at left
is digging an emplacement for a light machine gun.

Mazagan, Morocco, November 16, 1942.
American troops, moving toward the front in
a half-track, pass a French garrison.

Arzev, North Africa, December 4, 1942. The 1st Ranger Battalion moves up in double time.

December 12, 1942. U.S. troops move up a hill under fire.

From left to right: Pfc. J. Kalme, Pvt. D. Heck, Pvt. P. G. Kenneghue, and Pvt. G. R. Hayth in North Africa. January 19, 1943.

North Africa, February 20, 1943. A 105mm gun crew shelling enemy positions.

American tank moves up to strengthen Allied positions against German attacks. February 20, 1943.

Captain G. W. Meade in an M-4 tank. North Africa, February 24, 1943.

Tunisia, February 24, 1943. The crew of an antiaircraft gun, mounted on a half-track, prepare to fire on attacking enemy bombers.

Retreating Afrika Korps Germans have blown up a railroad bridge to delay American pursuit. March 13, 1943.

An Italian fighter shot down near Derna by American fighters.

North Africa, 1943. A soldier in a foxhole. The dust in the background is made by German tanks trying to turn the flank of the 1st Infantry Division at El Guettar. They are hit by artillery fire and knocked out.

Company D, 18th Infantry of the 1st Division, dig in the El Guettar hills during the U.S. advance to Gabee.

Sousse, Tunisia, April 1943. A repair unit replacing a damaged track on an M-4 tank.

North Africa, April 1943. German Mark VI tanks knocked out by U.S. artillery fire and bombing.

LCI's loading troops in Tunisia. The landing craft are manned by Navy and Coast Guard crews. Each LCI was loaded with 200 GI's. These soldiers participated in the linkup with the British 8th Army on April 7, 1943.

Tunisia, El Guettar sector. Photograph taken on April 8, 1943. On Macknassy Road an Allied tank and truck convoy return from a battle. A change in the weather brought dust and cold, which was tough on tired troops.

Tunisia, El Guettar sector, April 11, 1943. Part of a convoy of the 1st Armored Division moves back to a rest area after mopping up enemy opposition. A German Me-109 fighter was shot down by U.S. antiaircraft fire.

Mateur, Tunisia, April 26, 1943. The tracks of a destroyed Mark VI German tank. American GI's move toward Mateur.

Mateur, Tunisia, April 26, 1943. A knocked-out Afrika Korps Mark VI tank is passed by a fast-moving U.S. armored car.

Bizerte, Tunisia, May 7, 1943. The 60th
Infantry Battalion advances up a hill 10
miles from Bizerte. A forced march brought
them to the outskirts of the city at 2:30 P.M.

Bizerte, May 8, 1943. American GI's hug the
walls as they enter Bizerte.

Bizerte. After difficult street fighting, Bizerte
fell on May 9, 1943.

Lancia, Tripoli, May 18, 1943. A U.S. tank "graveyard" has become the base of an ordnance unit. The tanks cannot be repaired due to the lack of spare parts.

Algeria. Port Aux Poule, near Oran, June 6, 1943. The 36th Division attacks with a flame-thrower and grenades under enemy fire from a pillbox. The unit is Company F, 142nd Infantry.

Algeria, 1943. Antiaircraft fire during an air raid by Luftwaffe bombers.

Algeria, 1943. U.S. Rangers crash through a door after a sniper hiding in the house.

Tunisia, May 8, 1943. Sniper fire pins down GI's as a tank tries to blow concealed Germans out of the damaged buildings.

Algiers, North Africa. Black smoke rises from an exploding ship in the harbor, 8/4/43.

Epitaph for the Afrika Korps. The sun sets on a German cemetery. Photograph taken in 1944.

CHAPTER 3 STALEMATE IN ITALY: CASSINO AND ANZIO

"I had hoped we were hurling a wildcat on shore, but all we got was a stranded whale."

—Winston Churchill on the stalemate at Anzio.

Three days after Christmas, 1943, in the darkened bedroom of a sprawling villa deep in the Moroccan desert, Winston Churchill stirred from a brief, fitful sleep.

Rising, he moved unsteadily to a window and pulled back the drape. The room was flooded with blazing sunlight. Slowly, his eyes adjusted to a familiar vista—miles of sculptured sand dunes stretching away from Marrakesh as far as the eye could see.

Churchill knew the scene well. Almost a year earlier, following the Casablanca Conference, he and President Roosevelt had spent several delightful days at the same villa. But he had been healthy then, and vigorous, not enfeebled by the lingering effects of pneumonia as he was now.

Turning, he eased himself into a stuffed chair. Troubling thoughts, interrupted by his brief nap, quickly returned.

The Anglo-American campaign in Italy had fallen into a seemingly hopeless stalemate. The country's mountainous terrain and rain-swollen rivers had seen the Allied advance bog down midway up the boot, at the peninsula's narrowest point, before a German defensive position known as the Gustav Line. The front, facing the town of Cassino and its mountaintop monastery, threatened to remain static well into spring.

In his concern, Churchill had championed a plan for amphibious landings at the port of Anzio, 100 miles south of Rome, aimed at seizing the Italian capital and breaking the stalemate at Cassino as well.

It was a bold, risky maneuver. Only days before, he had received reluctant approval for the operation from key Allied leaders.

One serious problem remained. With Operation Overlord—the invasion of Normandy—rapidly approaching, not to mention Anvil, a simultaneous incursion into southern France, there were not enough landing craft available to mount the Anzio invasion.

But Churchill was determined that the landings, code named Shingle, take place. Days before, he had telegraphed a plea to President Roosevelt asking that 56 landing boats be retained in the Mediterranean for use at Anzio. Without them, his plan was doomed. Now, he awaited Roosevelt's reply.

The late afternoon sun slowly edged its way to his chair and the ailing prime minister rose feebly to draw the drapes against it. He was amazed at how weak he felt—infuriated that he was ill at such a critical time in the war.

He knew that Shingle had become an obsession. But with the Italians out of the war and German resistance stiffening noticeably, the Cassino stalemate simply had to be broken. Surely Roosevelt would recognize that a renewed offensive in Italy would almost certainly draw German troops out of western

Europe, thereby helping the impending French invasions. Or would he?

Churchill watched as a military staff car pulled up before the villa. Moments later, the anxious British leader held Roosevelt's reply. The answer was yes. The 56 boats would be retained for the operation at Anzio.

Telegram in hand, Churchill hobbled back to his bed and lay back. The tension seemed to drain from him. He closed his eyes, certain that when sleep came it would be deep and peaceful.

Lt. Gen. Clark, commanding the American V Army, trained his glasses on the mountaintop Benedictine monastery overlooking the town of Cassino and the valley of the Rapido. Even on this rare sunny day in early January, the imposing 6th-century structure looked grim and forbidding.

Clark now focused on the swirling Rapido River as it snaked its way across the valley. Beyond it lay the towns of St. Angelo, built on a bluff overlooking the river, and Cassino, peacefully nestled against the distant mountains.

Were he a tourist, Mark Clark would have considered it a stunning sight. But he was a soldier and the scene only filled him with dread.

The prize that lay beyond the mountains was the Liri Valley and its two highways leading north to Rome. Their capture would enable him to use armor effectively for the first time in the four-month Italian campaign. But first, the Rapido would have to be conquered and the mountaintop monastery, dominating his positions, taken by direct assault. No simple task.

Clark again raised his glasses toward the monastery, recalling the words of a wise military tactician who said, "The secret of mountain warfare is to devoutly avoid it." He focused on the distant towers, wondering if some bored German sentry might be looking back at him, wishing that the damned place had never been built.

With the necessary landing craft now available, plans for the Anzio invasion moved forward at full speed. The assault was assigned to two divisions—the British 2nd and the U.S. 3rd. Along with British commandos and a battalion of American Rangers, they would comprise the Sixth Corps under Maj. Gen. John P. Lucas, an American.

Since the operation was tied in with a simultaneous offensive at Cassino, Gen. Clark selected the U.S. 36th Division, led by Maj. Gen. F. L. Walker, to make an assault crossing of the Rapido, setting up an attack on Monte Cassino while diverting attention from the landings at Anzio.

The hazards of river crossings were well known to Gen. Walker. As a battalion commander in France during World War I, he had seen 1,200 Americans slaughter 10,000 Germans trying to ford the Marne. The Rapido crossing, he knew, could be equally disastrous. In order to support units already across the river, tanks would have to be brought over quickly. But the raging river threatened to resist all attempts at putting bridges across. And his engineers would be forced to work with German guns looking down on them from the heights. Walker pleaded for more time to plan but Clark was adamant. The attack, he said, would commence on January 20th.

Gen. Walker's two-regiment effort to cross the Rapido was, as predicted, a disaster. While elements of both regiments managed to reach the German side, tank-bearing Bailey bridges could not be erected in the fast-flowing stream. With his armor stranded on the wrong side as feared, Walker watched in horror as his troops already across were cut to pieces by the 14th Panzer Corps of Nazi Gen. von Veitinghoff's X Army. During two days of ferocious combat, the 36th suffered more than 1,000 dead and missing.

In a later answer to critics of the operation, Gen. Clark said, "If I am to be accused of something, thank God it's for attacking, not retreating."

Two days later, at 0200 on the clear, still night of January 22, 1944, the 6th Corps went ashore on the beaches at Anzio and Nettuno. By midnight 36,000 men were ashore. Surprise had been complete. Less than 1,000 troops of Gen. von Mackensen's XIV Army had opposed the landings.

The following morning, standing before his special armor-plated quarters aboard the flagship *Biscayne*, Gen. John Lucas, an ever-present corncob pipe clutched in his teeth, watched as mountains of equipment piled up on the Anzio shore.

At 54, Lucas seemed older than his years. Slow and cautious— some said pathologically so—he thought about the orders he had received from Gen. Clark: SEIZE AND SECURE A BEACHHEAD IN THE VICINITY OF ANZIO, THEN ADVANCE TOWARD THE ALBAN HILLS. Rome had not been mentioned.

Lucas was fully aware that Gen. Sir Harold Alexander, commanding all Allied land forces in Italy, had announced the aim of the operation as the quick seizure of Rome followed by a rapid advance to the Alban hills. This would cut the two main arteries leading south and threaten the rear of Von Veitinghoff's army on the Cassino front.

But Clark had said *toward* the Alban Hills, not *to* them. And he had said nothing about Rome. To John Lucas, the orders were vague if not contradictory.

Openly critical of the Anzio plan from the beginning, he had resented Churchill's bullish tactics in getting them approved. With reference to the prime minister's part in planning the ill-fated Gallipoli operation during World War I, Lucas had told his associates, "This one has the same odor—and the same coach is on the bench."

Those around him felt that sufficient strength was already ashore at Anzio to strike out boldly against Von Mackensen. But Lucas refused to be steamrollered. When the heavy artillery and additional tanks were ashore, he would consider an attack. Not before.

The general drew heavily on his pipe, listening as the chilling thump of German artillery moved closer. The time for attack would come, he knew. But only John Lucas would decide when that would be.

To the south, Mark Clark vigorously pressed his Cassino attacks. Walker's 34th Division managed to gain a tenuous foothold across the Rapido. But an accompanying attack by Gen. Alphonse Juin's French Expeditionary Force, intended to outflank the German positions with an advance through the mountains, met with little success. Cassino and its mountaintop monastery continued to resist every Allied effort to break into the valley.

At Anzio, under extreme pressure from Gen. Clark, John Lucas launched his first attack on January 29, 1944. Gen. Lucien Truscott's U.S. 3rd Division moved on Cisterna while the British

1st attacked Campoleone. American Rangers and a joint U.S.-Canadian Special Forces group joined the action.

Lucas's week-long caution now proved his undoing. Instead of the scattered Panzergrenadiere units that had faced the beachhead when the landings took place, his troops ran up against eight crack German divisions rushed to the area from France, Germany, and Yugoslavia. The Allied attacks were stopped cold.

The beachhead was now under constant attack by giant railway guns nicknamed "Anzio Express" and "Anzio Annie." With a German counteroffensive looming, Lucas was ordered to reinforce the area and prepare for defense.

In Berlin, Adolf Hitler was ecstatic. "I see an Italian Dunkirk in the making," he was reported to have said.

Preparing to attack at Anzio, Gen. von Mackensen wired his Führer, "I am ready to throw the Allied invaders back into the sea."

Alarmed by the situation at Anzio, Gens. Clark and Alexander met in emergency session. They agreed that action at Cassino would have to be intensified in order to relieve the pressure at Anzio. Alexander detached a New Zealand Corps from the British 8th Army, operating on Italy's east coast, to assist the Americans. Plans were put in place for renewed attacks against the Gustav Line.

On February 3rd, Gen. von Mackensen's XIV Army launched a series of determined assaults against the Anzio beachhead, his major effort focused on Campoleone. When the British 1st Division began falling back, the situation quickly turned critical. The just-landed British 56th Division hurried into the line. Rumor had it that the entire 6th Corps might have to be evacuated.

On February 7th, Von Mackensen briefly took the key town of Aprila. But the British, realizing that the entire beachhead was about to collapse, fought their way back into the city. Pulling back, Von Mackensen switched his efforts toward Carraceto.

As the battle raged, some news correspondents, convinced that a great Allied defeat was at hand, left Anzio. While Lucas fumed at what he called "alarmist rumors," comments harshly critical of the general's "inertia" continued to be heard. Said one British general, "We'll lose the beachhead unless Lucas goes."

When intelligence reported that an all-out German attack could be expected on February 16th, Gen. Clark rushed to Anzio from Cassino. Gen. Alexander joined him there.

With his two somber commanders looking on, John Lucas readied his last-ditch defense. Anticipating eventual relief, he wrote in his diary, *I have done my best. My conscience is clear.*

Standing at the center of the cavernous Benedictine abbey at Cassino, Lt. Col. Julius Schlagel watched as several dozen German soldiers finished sealing the last of many crates containing the monastery's priceless treasures.

Schlagel, a middle-aged staff officer, had seen the handwriting on the wall. The Allies could not allow the stalemate to continue. They would destroy the centuries-old abbey, which they believed to be an observation post key to the area's defense.

A Roman Catholic and an art connoisseur, Schlagel knew this to be false. Field Marshal Kesselring himself had ordered a "free zone" established around the abbey. German combat troops were forbidden to approach closer than 300 meters. But who would believe that? It was sadly inevitable. The beautiful monastery would be the war's next victim.

Schlagel, who hated the war with a passion, realized that his rank, perhaps even his life was at risk. Without proper authority, he had convinced the monastery's aged abbot to let him rescue the abbey's irreplaceable art treasures. Even now, military vehicles that he had falsely requisitioned were preparing to transport his precious crates over the 100-mile route to Rome. He worried that Allied bombers or fighters might attack the convoy. But there was no other way; he would take his chances on the road north.

As the distant sounds of battle echoed through the valley, Julius Schlagel hurried his men, anxious to see the last of the paintings and art treasures out of the building.

Later, standing beneath the spacious dome, his eyes drifted over the abbey's sun-splashed beauty for one last time. It was too heartbreaking to think about. American bombs would soon reduce the place to smoking rubble. This historic, holy shrine, Schlagel knew, was as doomed as his beloved Fatherland.

The irrevocable decision was taken. The monastery must fall. Mark Clark opposed its destruction. Gen. Bernard Freyberg, commanding the about-to-attack New Zealand Corps, insisted on it. So did Gen. Alexander, who said, "Bricks and mortar, no matter how venerable, cannot be allowed to bear against human lives."

With the 34th Division's gallant efforts to take the abbey having ended in failure—at one point they were less than a thousand yards from their goal—Freyberg's 4th Indian Division prepared to attack behind the monastery's bombing.

At 0930 on February 15th, attacking in two waves, 229 American bombers, dropping more than 400 tons of explosives, leveled the abbey atop Monte Cassino, one of the shrines of western Christian culture. German troops quickly infiltrated the smoking ruins. They were now able to observe the slightest movement from below.

For three days, men of the 4th Indian and New Zealand 2nd divisions attempted to capture key enemy positions on the mountain as well as crack the defenses of Cassino town. The Germans thwarted every effort by Freyberg's forces. The battle ended with Von Veitinghoff's X Army still in firm control of the area.

On February 16th, Gen. von Mackensen hurled his XIV Army against the Anzio beachhead. At Hitler's personal request, the elite Panzer Lehr Regiment led the attack. But when Allied artillery massacred their ranks, they broke and fled. A subsequent attack by the Hermann Göring Division at Cisterna was also beaten back with heavy German losses.

In the west, the British 56th and U.S. 45th divisions joined the battle. Allied bombers pounded Von Mackensen's positions. Lorries were soon piled high with the German dead.

As the powerful enemy attacks continued into the 17th, the Allies found their backs to The Flyover—a viaduct bridge that was their last defensible position before Anzio itself. In the rear, sensitive papers were ordered burned. The end seemed near.

On the 19th, however, when a tank attack led by the 1st Armored Division's fearless commander, Gen. Ernest Harmon, broke through Von Mackensen's positions, the exhausted Germans gave up. For the moment, the beachhead was safe. But

Lucas's troops now lacked the strength to attack. A stalemate was in the offing.

At 8 P.M. on February 22nd, in a basement command post, Mark Clark relieved John P. Lucas as commander of the 6th Corps. Maj. Gen. Lucien Truscott was selected to replace him. The following day, after saying goodbye to "the best damned soldiers that ever lived," the disillusioned Lucas left Anzio. The target of bitter criticism, he would die shortly after the war.

With the Anzio front now quiet, plans were made to break the stalemate at Cassino.

On March 12, 1944, a massive Allied bombing of Cassino town was followed by the second assault of Freyberg's New Zealand Corps. The half-mile-long town was shrouded in smoke and dust. But the German defenders, having quickly recovered from the effects of the massive bombing, resisted fanatically. Fighting in the cold and rain, Freyberg's troops struggled for every foot of the smouldering town. At the same time, Ghurka troops, who had captured a mountain position called Hangman's Hill, defended it heroically and at great cost. But when Lt. Gen. Heidrich's 1st Parachute Division refused to be dislodged from Cassino, the entire effort failed.

The final Allied operation designed to break the stalemates at Cassino and Anzio was code named Diadem. It called for a breakout of V and VIII army units along a 20-mile Cassino front. A major effort by Truscott's 6th Corps at Anzio would follow the Cassino action. Diadem was to be no storming of a single point, but a broad, well-planned offensive on two fronts.

With the American V Army on the left and the British VIII Army on the right, Operation Diadem was launched at Cassino on May 12th. Truscott's breakout at Anzio was to await General Clark's order.

On the coast, the American II Corps got off to a slow start. To the east, General Anders's Polish II Corps had its initial attacks against Monastery Hill thrown back. But Gen. Alphonse Juin's French Corps, attacking through the mountains, made rapid progress, capturing Monte Maio and commanding the road network leading to the Liri Valley. The pressure exerted by Juin's stunning victory was such that Heidrich's Parachute Division was ordered to fall back from Cassino to avoid capture. At long last the vaunted Gustav Line had been breached.

Anders's Polish legions, having suffered horrendous casualties in repeated efforts to take Monastery Hill, finally entered the abbey's ruins on the morning of May 18th. A handful of Heidrich's men who had stayed behind, most of them wounded, lay down their arms. The Polish flag was raised over what remained of the shattered shrine.

On May 23rd, as the V and VIII armies continued their rapid advance to the north, Gen. Truscott began his drive to break out of the Anzio area. He had been instructed to seize Valmontone and cut Route #7, Gen. von Veitinghoff's escape route.

Cisterna fell on the 25th. That same day, elements of the 6th Corps and the V Army linked up. After 125 days, the siege of Anzio was over.

Although Truscott's capture of Valmontone would have trapped the German X Army, Mark Clark now had his eyes on

Rome. Determined that American troops would have that prize, intent upon denying it to Alexander and the British, he ordered a stunned Truscott to veer north and strike out for the capital. Only a light force was sent to attack Valmontone. When that weakened group was unable to accomplish the task in time, the fleeing 10th Army poured through the city and escaped north.

Mark Clark entered Rome in triumph on June 5, 1944, hours behind the retreating Germans. At midnight, he stood on the banks of the Tiber, thinking of the long agonies at Anzio and Cassino, reveling in the glorious victory of his GI's whose bloody nine-month struggle up the Italian boot had at last found its reward. Rome was theirs and the free world was in celebration.

But Clark knew that their moment of elation would quickly pass. At that very moment, American airborne assault troops were flying over the French coast. Within hours, the earthshaking events at Normandy Beach would seize the world's headlines. And rightfully so.

But that was tomorrow. Tonight was his—a time, however brief, to savor the sweet nectar of victory.

Gela, Sicily, July 10, 1943. D-Day on Red Beach at Gela, Sicily. LCI's and barges unloading troops and supplies.

Gela, Sicily. Axis planes bombing the invasion force heading for the beach.

American tank and infantry units advancing to meet Nazi counterattack. Gela, Sicily, July 1943.

Reinforcements arrive on Red Beach at Gela, Sicily. July 10, 1943.

Gela, Sicily, July 11, 1943. A U.S. ammunition ship blows up after taking a direct hit from a Nazi J-87 dive bomber.

General George Patton comes ashore at Gela to command his troops on the spot. July 11, 1943.

Sicily, July 12, 1943. Men debarking from lighter on sector of Red Beach, between Gela and Scoglitti.

U.S. infantry move inland from Red Beach under enemy rifle fire.

Sicily, July 14, 1943. Troops of the 41st Armored Infantry Regiment attacking German snipers near Canicatti.

Sicily, July 1943. A 155mm cannon being moved into position to blunt a German counterattack.

A U.S. Armored troop carrier moves through Palma, as civilians watch. Sicily, July 1943.

A U.S. supply train burns after an explosion from an "unidentified" source. Sicily, July 1943.

Agrigento Airfield, July 25, 1943. Gen. Patton talking to Pvt. Frank A. Reed of East Dephen, Mass., of the 7th Infantry Regiment of the 3rd Infantry Division. Reed and other wounded GI's were awaiting evacuation to hospitals in North Africa.

Sicily, July 28, 1943. The 1st Infantry Division at Nicosia with captured German soldiers. They were temporarily held at the City Hall.

Messina, Sicily, August 6, 1943. U.S. troops move through the still-smoking ruins of the city, August 6, 1943.

August 7, 1943. In Sicily, a U.S. tank put ashore in the rear of the German defenses plunges ahead to engage the enemy.

Sicily, August 14, 1943. A 105mm howitzer firing at German positions.

August 1943. Gen. Patton looks at Italian
prisoners in the town center of Gela, Sicily.

August 14, 1943. U.S. troops march into
Gioiosa, Sicily, following the capture of Messina.

The 45th Infantry Division moving through
Messina. August 17, 1943.

October 4, 1943. 45th Infantry Division troops walk through the streets of Beneven, Italy. The GI's are from the 45th's 12th Engineers.

Cassino, Italy, November 7, 1943. A German Focke-Wulf 190 fighter hits a truck carrying cans of fuel oil. Some of the cans lie on the road.

Cassino, November 7, 1943. German fighter strafes a U.S. convoy.

Troops landing on the Anzio beachhead, January 22, 1944. The landing was designed to relieve pressure on the Volturno-Cassino front by landing in the German rear areas.

5th Army troops and equipment pour ashore at Anzio.

January 22, 1944. South of Anzio, vehicles and equipment debark from landing craft.

January 22, 1944. Troops wading ashore on the beachhead at Anzio.

Anzio Beachhead. M-7 self-propelled guns of the 45th Infantry Division fire on enemy positions.

An infantry patrol engages in close fighting near Anzio.

February 6, 1944. Artillery from a U.S. battery shells Cassino. Monte Cassino monastery stands atop hill.

February 15, 1944. Blasting Nazis holed up in the Benedictine monastery of Monte Cassino.

San Pietro, February 24, 1944. Ammunition dump explodes after being struck by German shells.

U.S. infantry move into San Pietro after heavy shelling. February 1944.

February 29, 1944. Combat engineers use salvage rails to build machine-gun emplacements.

The ruins of the town of Cassino after its capture.

A photograph of the ruined Monte Cassino Abbey at the end of the siege. Little remains of the original monastery. February 1944.

The U.S. Military Cemetery at Caronia, Sicily, 1944.

Near Livorno, May 1944. Protective coloration. A V Army medium tank takes shelter in a crevice in the rubble to avoid detection by enemy observation posts, which would order heavy shellfire.

Mark Clark congratulates Lt. Roland J. Gagnon and two of his men for outstanding bravery in the assault on the port city of Livorno.

Japanese-American infantrymen of the 100th Battalion, 34th Division, move along a dusty road in the Velletri area. May 28, 1944.

A unique observation post behind an Italian straw house. A 45th Division observer watches tanks and infantry move forward to their objective, May 29, 1944.

Tanks of the 1st Armored division gather to spearhead the 45th Infantry division's push northward toward Rome, May 1944.

Black troops of Company "I" 3rd Battalion, 370th Infantry Regiment move against the enemy.

June 2, 1944. A dead German soldier lies beside the road as American tanks pass through the town of Velletri.

June 4, 1944. The spearhead of a task force drives on to take Rome. To the left of the road can be seen a knocked-out M-4 tank hit by a self-propelled 88mm gun in the vicinity of Rome.

June 4, 1944. A tank destroyer blasts a German machine-gun emplacement in a wall on a Rome street.

The Fifth Army enters Rome. They were greeted by huge smiling crowds along the route.

Rome's Ciampino Airport, formerly held by the Nazis, had been heavily bombed during Allied offensive.

June 6, 1944. The Germans used Littoria Airport near Rome after it had been severely bombed by Allied bombers.

Members of the Japanese-American 100th Infantry Battalion rest in the center of Livorno, July 19, 1944.

July 19, 1944. Among the bombing casualties in Rome was the beautiful Church of San Lorento.

A tank moves through Arcora, greeted by a crowd.

A jeep convoy drives down the Via Toscolana in Rome.

The U.S. tanks move on, and Romans begin the cleanup.

Two American GI's at the Colosseum.

A battalion composed of American troops of Japanese descent marches through the town of Vada, where Gen. Mark W. Clark, CG of the 5th Army, presented them the Presidential unit citation for outstanding action in combat. July 27, 1944.

Pontederra, September 1, 1944. The 92nd Infantry Division crosses the Arno and begins scaling the muddy riverbank toward the German positions.

September 4, 1944. American vehicles crossing the Arno River north of Cascina.

Futa Pass, September 27, 1944. Troops of the 363rd Regiment of the 91st Infantry Division carry rations for troops on the Gothic Line.

December 5, 1944, on the way to Bologna. A 1st Armored Division gun crew scores a hit on the German stronghold at Monterumic. American infantry are only a few hundred yards below the bursts.

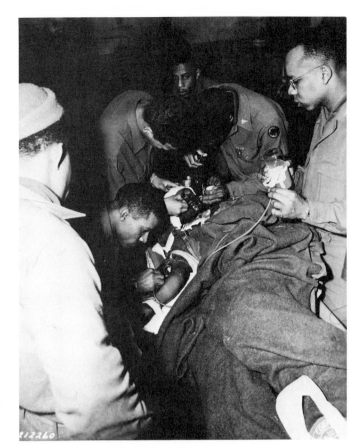

A wounded American soldier receives blood plasma and treatment from a black medical unit of the 92nd Infantry Division.

Company B, 86th Mountain Infantry Regiment of the 10th Mountain Infantry Division patrol, moves out carrying snowshoes. Deep snow in the mountains makes them necessary. January 10, 1945.

Sonmocolonia front, January 10, 1945. Company C, 365th Infantry Regiment of the 92nd Infantry Division, is pinned down by a German sniper who infiltrated through the U.S. lines.

South Clemente, January 18, 1945. Members of the 337th Infantry of the 85th Division repair a supply trail in the Apennine mountains. Rifles are handy in case of enemy attack.

Spigvana, Italy, January 21, 1945. Ski patrol loads gear into a Weasel and will be towed to the take-off point for a patrol into enemy territory. The patrol is made up of men from the 86th Regiment, 10th Mountain Division.

Vincinetta area, February 8, 1945. B Battery of the 616th Field Artillery Pack Howitzer Battalion sends rounds of 75mm shells into German positions high in the Apennines. The unit is from the 10th Mountain Division.

87th Mountain Infantry of the 10th Mountain Division of the V Army adds another victory to its score. Corona, Italy, February 20, 1945.

Serrasiccia tramway, February 21, 1945. Artillery observers descend a 1,156-meter mountain via a tramway built by Company D of the 126th Mountain Engineers, 10th Mountain Division. The tramway was also used to remove wounded from the mountain and for bringing up supplies and ammunition.

Easter Sunday, March 1, 1945, Castelfiorentino Military Cemetery. Maj. Gen. Edward M. Almond, CG, 92nd Infantry Division, 5th Army, lays a wreath at the grave of one of the Division's dead.

A tank of the 1st Armored Division. The M-4 tank has just been repaired and is moving out toward the front.

H. Della Vedetta, March 3, 1945. The 87th Mountain Infantry of the 10th Mountain Division dash over the crest of a hill. The German has been killed by artillery fire. H. Della Vedetta is near the Modena-Poretta highway.

March 3, 1945. A tank destroyer protects 10th Mountain Division troops from sniper fire. This occurred at Castel D'Aiano.

H. Della Vedetta. Fighter bombers from the air support the attack of 10th Mountain Division troops on the Poretta-Moderna highway. The German position is 200 yards away. March 3, 1945.

Po Valley, April 1945. U.S. troops move
rapidly through the city of Vicenza.

Seravezza, April 8, 1945. A 75mm howitzer
mounted on a light tank gives support fire to
the 442nd Infantry Regiment.

Campidallo, April 15, 1945, German prisoners taken by the 10th Mountain Division are
marched into a stockade behind enemy lines.

April 20, 1945. Troops of the 91st Infantry Division and tanks of the 6th South African Division move in on Casalecchio.

Ostiglia, on the Po River, April 24, 1945. The 351st Infantry of the 88th Division get covering fire from a 57mm antitank gun as the unit crosses the Po.

April 24, 1945. Alligators transport men of the 3rd Battalion of the 351st Infantry of the 88th Division across the Po at Ostiglia.

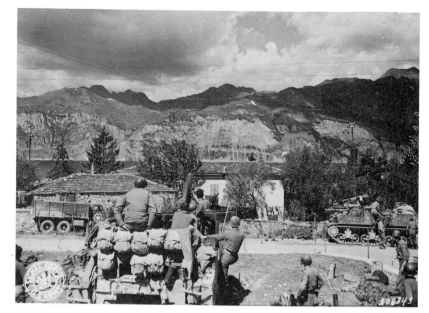

Lake Garda, near Gargnano, April 29, 1945. A battalion of the 10th Mountain Division fires at a German convoy with a 105mm gun mounted on a full-tracked gun carriage.

Brennero, Italy, May 18, 1945. 103rd Division, U.S. Seventh Army, wrecks the railroad yards at the Brenner Pass. Precision bombing left adjacent buildings intact.

CHAPTER 4 D-DAY: THE NORMANDY INVASION

"O.K., we'll go."

—General Eisenhower's decision to launch D-day.

Field Marshal Erwin Rommel, seated peacefully in the rear of his black convertible Horch, watched with growing pleasure the further deterioration of the French weather. The misty rain that now blurred the passing countryside told him that an Allied invasion would not occur for at least a week.

Rommel was grateful for the unexpected respite from his duties at La Roche Guyon, headquarters of Army Group B, north of Paris. It gave him time to visit Herrlingen, his home on the Danube, where his wife was to observe her birthday two days hence. He welcomed the opportunity to be with Lucie Maria and their 15-year-old son, Manfred.

The trip was not without its dark side, however. Rommel had also scheduled an urgent meeting with the Führer at Berchtesgaden, one that promised to be particularly stormy.

No longer the dashing and optimistic armored commander who had raged through the Libyan desert 18 months before, the 53-year-old field marshal knew that the next few weeks of the war were critical. An Allied invasion was imminent. When it came, it had to be stopped at the beaches within the first 48 hours. Otherwise, all was lost. But the Führer had stubbornly refused every request to move the reserve armored divisions closer to the Atlantic Wall, preferring to hold them well inland until the real invasion site had been committed. He was worried that the first strike might be a diversion—that the major landings would come elsewhere. But his restrictions on the mobile armored reserves were nothing short of national suicide. This foolish strategy reminded Rommel of Frederick the Great's observation, "He who tries to defend everything, defends nothing."

As the Horch, buffeted by a rising wind, motored toward Germany, Rommel reviewed his assets.

Since the German defeat in North Africa, he had worked tirelessly to improve the defenses of the Atlantic Wall. His two armies, the VII and XV, poised between the Cotentin peninsula and Holland, were set to repel Eisenhower's invaders. Coastal batteries and fortifications, except for some last-minute work along the Normandy coast, were in place. He was particularly proud of the beachfront obstacles, many of which he had personally designed. True, when the invasion came, Göring's battered Luftwaffe would be of little help. But Rommel was confident that the coastal defenses would give him time to destroy the Allied landing with a lightning thrust of his armor. That is, if he could convince Hitler—a challenge he regarded with no great enthusiasm.

As the Horch crossed into Germany, the weather seemed to brighten. Rommel was not concerned. Hadn't the chief Luftwaffe meteorologist in Paris told him that the high winds and rain would persist for several days? Eisenhower would be foolish to attack without clear skies and a high tide. Whatever else the American was, Rommel thought, he was no gambler.

Later that same day, June 4, 1944, Gen. Eisenhower, Supreme Commander of Allied Forces in Europe, stepped from the trailer that served as his living quarters into a rain-lashed wood outside of Portsmouth, England. He paused to look beyond the wind-swept treetops, gloomily seeking some sign that the front might move on. Finding none, he turned up his collar and, hunched against the elements, walked toward Allied Naval Headquarters at nearby Southwick House and the gravest decision of his life.

Thirty minutes later, the Allied invasion leaders listened as Group Captain J. N. Stagg, Operation Overlord's chief meteorologist, briefed them on the upcoming weather. Eisenhower was particularly tense, having postponed the landings for 24 hours the night before.

Stagg's predictions seemed quite simple. While the present front would linger for several days, there would be a window of improving weather beginning midday on June 5th and lasting well into the 6th. Then a rapid deterioration was expected.

Eisenhower shifted nervously. There it was. He could launch his attack on the Normandy coast on June 6th, under barely tolerable conditions, or delay it until later in June, perhaps even July. Men and ships were already at sea. Calling them back presented massive logistical problems, not to mention grave security risks. And Hitler, it was said, was ready to launch a new and deadly self-propelled aerial bomb against England. The general considered what such a weapon might do to his over-loaded invasion ports across from the French coast.

When Stagg finished his briefing, the group was polled. The consensus was that the gamble had to be taken. But the final decision was Eisenhower's. As the others looked on in stony silence, he weighed the facts, then ordered that the landings proceed at 0630 on June 6th. "I don't see how we can do anything else," he said.

Long after midnight, a restless Eisenhower lay, fully clothed, on his bed. Heavy rain hammered against the trailer's metal roof. In a few hours, after a final check with Stagg, he would confirm his decision to launch Operation Overlord.

Now he thought only of his opponents—Hitler, Von Runstedt, Rommel—and wondered whether his elaborate deception had worked.

More than a year earlier, he had launched Operation Fortitude, a program designed to mislead the Germans into believing that the invasion would be launched against the Pas de Calais, a few miles across the Channel from southeast England. There, Hitler had massed his greatest defenses, including the powerful XV Army. If that considerable force could be kept tied down, it would greatly improve Allied chances for success. Hitler, Eisenhower hoped, would believe that the Normandy landings were only a feint—that the real attack would come at the Pas de Calais.

With enormous help from British intelligence and the use of "turned" German agents, the Allies had created a fictitious First Army Group, supposedly led by Gen. Patton. To enhance the deception, dummy headquarters, empty barracks, bogus air-fields, plus tanks, planes, and landing craft fabricated from rubber, wood, and paper, had been spread all across the fields of Kent. Patton was frequently seen in the area. Some actual personnel and equipment added to the authenticity of this notional army group.

The Germans, it seemed, *had* been taken in. Reports received from intelligence suggested that Hitler and most of his generals were convinced that the hated Patton would lead the assault against the Pas de Calais. As a result, the XV Army remained securely fixed in the area.

Fortitude had been a gutsy attempt at deception. Now, barely 36 hours before the big show was set to begin, Eisenhower tossed nervously, hoping his gamble would pay off.

The greatest amphibious operation in history began as more than 5,000 Allied ships gathered at an English Channel rendez-vous area code named "Piccadilly Circus" before proceeding in 10 columns toward the Normandy coast.

At country airfields all across England, pilots and crews attended their briefings before taking off to support the long-awaited assault on Fortress Europe.

At Newbury Race Course, on the Channel coast, men of Maj. Gen. Maxwell Taylor's 101st Airborne Division, faces blackened, waited to depart for preinvasion drops behind Utah Beach, one of the two American landing sites. Before leaving they held a final, emotional meeting with Eisenhower.

At other locations in England, Maj. Gen. Matthew B. Ridgeway's 82nd Airborne Division also took off to join the 101st in the perilous night drops behind enemy lines.

Along the Atlantic Wall, sleepy German soldiers, manning their positions, hardly bothered to check the fog-smeared Channel horizon. The weather, they knew, precluded any landing attempt. It promised to be just another dreary night on the coast of Normandy.

The Western Task Force, the American half of the invasion convoy, approached its two invasion beaches, designated Utah and Omaha. Located on either side of the Vire estuary, they were to be assaulted by troops of Gen. Bradley's U.S. I Army.

Utah Beach, at the base of the Cotentin Peninsula, was on the right or west. Maj. Gen. J. Lawton Collins's 7th Corps was selected to make the attack. The 4th Infantry Division would lead the way.

Omaha Beach, a five-mile stretch of the Normandy coast running between Vierville and Colleville, would be attacked by Maj. Gen. Leonard Gerow's 5th Corps. Elements of the U.S. 29th Division and the veteran U.S. 1st—the Big Red One—would make the assault.

Farther east, the British landing area extended along 25 miles of the French coast from Port-en-Bessin to the mouth of the Orne River. The beaches, west to east, were designated Gold, Juno, and Sword. They would be assaulted by three divisions of the British II Army. Airborne units were already landing to secure vital points in the area of Caen.

All ground troops in the assault phase of Overlord were under the command of British Gen. Montgomery.

Shortly after midnight on June 6th, American airborne troops began landing behind Utah Beach. The wind and blinding rain made for tragic results.

Troopers of the 82nd and 101st Airborne divisions, ordered to secure key roads and bridges, were blown off course and widely scattered as they landed. Many drowned when they came down in flooded areas. Others landed at the center of St. Mère Eglise and were slaughtered by the waiting Germans. Still others died when their gliders crashed as the tense, inexperienced pilots groped for landing sites.

In the blackness of the French night, knots of men linked up to carry out their mission. Gen. Maxwell Taylor found himself in a group that included many officers but only a handful of enlisted men. "Never have so few been led by so many," he quipped.

Scores of firefights erupted. Hundreds of troopers were captured. Casualties topped 15 percent. While many of the airborne's goals were not achieved, the fear and confusion caused by their presence behind the lines more than compensated for the failed objectives of their mission.

Dawn broke over the stormy English Channel. Leaden skies looked down on the 5,339 ships of the invasion fleet gathered off the Normandy beaches.

All along the Atlantic Wall, astonished German sentries stared through the mist at the sprawling Allied armada. "The invasion, it's here!" one shouted. "They must be crazy," cried another.

Since midnight, in an effort to isolate the beaches, Allied bombers had carried out massive attacks against German communication points inland. The coastal batteries of the Atlantic Wall had also been subjected to sustained bombardment.

Now, the big ships of the Allied fleet opened up along a 60-mile stretch of the Normandy coast. At the same time, assault troops, British and American, bobbed about in the Channel's angry waters, anxiously awaiting their appointment with destiny.

Two hundred U.S. Rangers dashed for shore to assault Pointe du Hoe, a triangular cape located between Utah and Omaha beaches. At the top of a 117-foot cliff, the Germans were reported to have six 155mm guns capable of wreaking havoc on the American landings. The Rangers were to scale the cliff in the face of the enemy and destroy the guns. Their mission was considered suicidal. Said one Allied intelligence officer, "Three old ladies with brooms could keep those Rangers from climbing that cliff."

After successfully storming the height, the Rangers discovered that the 155's were nothing more than telephone poles, a clever German ruse. The actual guns were subsequently located and destroyed.

Off Utah Beach, 20 boats containing 600 men of the 4th Infantry Division's assault wave approached the Normandy shore. They were to establish a beachhead between Varreville and La Madeline, seize the causeways, then link up with troopers of the 82nd and 101st Airborne divisions waiting inland.

The amtrac ramps flopped down at precisely 0630 and the first American soldiers to land in France began wading toward land under heavy fire. They were led by Brig. Gen. Theodore Roosevelt, Jr., son of the former president.

As they reached the smoke-shrouded shore, many were hit and fell to the sand. German 88's opened up, blowing men apart. The stunned survivors raced for the cover offered by inland dunes.

With most of the beach obstacles having been cleared by army engineers and navy frogmen, the second wave approached. Gen. Roosevelt and other officers began urging the men inland, toward the causeway exits. Despite their casualties, the first troops of

"Lightning Joe" Collins's 7th Corps were successfully ashore.

At Omaha Beach, 10 miles to the east, tragedy loomed. The naval bombardment had had little effect on Rommel's concrete bunkers located behind the bluffs. In addition, the poor weather had caused B-24 pilots to drop their bombs harmlessly behind the beach, killing French civilians and cows, but few Germans. An attempt to launch 32 amphibious tanks a mile offshore backfired when the rough seas quickly swamped 29 of them. They went straight to the bottom with most of their crews. Omaha's assault wave would be without armor at a critical time.

The 29th Division's first wave encountered heavy fire as it approached the beach. Unknown to Allied intelligence, the crack 352nd Infantry Division had just moved into the area for training. Omaha's invaders would face strong opposition.

Fire from the shore batteries was deadly accurate. Landing craft exploded, throwing torn and bleeding men into the sea. Boats that reached the beach came under devastating fire. As the ramps came down, entire boatloads of men were killed before they could step ashore. Engineers and frogmen took horrendous casualties as they sought to clear beach obstacles under murderous fire. Wounded men floated helplessly in the surf. The dead and dying were everywhere. In the midst of the massacre, succeeding waves began piling up on the shore, presenting inviting targets for the German gunners. Some men were able to reach the seawall. There they crouched in shock, watching as others trying to gain the beach were decimated by the deadly German fire. The situation was desperate. The Omaha landings were in grave danger of failing.

At Gold, Juno, and Sword—the three beaches running between Le Hamel in the west and Ouistreham, at the mouth of the Orne River—the landings by Gen. Miles C. Dempsey's British II Army were delayed by weather and strong tides. Once ashore, however, Dempsey's troops began moving toward their principal objectives, Caen and Bayeux.

Fighting was particularly heavy at Sword Beach, where the British 3rd Infantry Division encountered concentrated fire from behind the landing site. Many of the beach obstacles had not been removed. Some first wave commando outfits suffered 90 percent casualties.

In the center, at Juno, the Canadian 3rd Infantry Division quickly overran the German beach defenses and pushed inland for several miles.

At Gold, the British 50th Division, storming ashore, found the way blocked by mined steel triangles imbedded in the beach. Many of the landing craft were destroyed when the heavy seas cast them upon these explosive obstacles. But opposition from the German defenders was surprisingly light and the troops set about neutralizing the German positions at Le Hamel.

As a whole, the British landings had been a success. By late morning, Dempsey's forces were moving toward a linkup with the British 6th Airborne in the vicinity of Caen.

At his headquarters at St. Germaine-en-Laye, outside of Paris, Field Marshal Gerd von Runstedt, Commander in Chief West, had reluctantly conceded that the Allied invasion had begun.

Earlier, when reports of parachute landings had caused him to be roused from a sound sleep, he had accepted the confusion of reports with some skepticism. An obvious feint, he thought, believing, like Hitler, that the principal landings would occur at the Pas de Calais.

As a safety measure, however, he had ordered the 21st Panzer Division to move toward Caen, the likely target of the attack. But now, with reports of landings all along the Normandy coast, the commander of OB West was convinced that the Allied landings were no diversion.

Incredible, he thought. Launching an invasion in this weather. But the crusty old field marshal, who had often won military laurels by employing the element of surprise, was now forced to admire a similar tactic in his enemy.

Von Runstedt had already alerted two of his crack reserve armored divisions—the Panzer Lehr and 12th SS—to be ready to roll. He also hoped to convince Hitler to release several units from the Pas de Calais. That, he knew, would be a battle all its own.

A telephone call from Berlin Headquarters brought an unexpected bottleneck. Von Runstedt was informed that only Hitler could release the two requested armored divisions. And the Führer, it seemed, was in a pill-induced sleep at Berchtesgaden and could not be disturbed.

Had the situation been less grave, Von Runstedt would have laughed. After all the planning, all the preparation, the Allied invasion threatened to succeed only because Hitler was snuggled warmly in his bed. It was too idiotic to think about. But nothing could be done. He would have to wait. And time, Von Runstedt knew, was the one thing he didn't have.

Aboard his flagship, *Augusta*, Gen. Omar Bradley, U.S. I Army Commander, pored over reports from the invasion beaches.

The landings at Utah had gone well. Men of Ray Barton's 4th Division were already moving inland through the causeway exits. Succeeding waves were coming ashore virtually unhampered. Barton confidently predicted an evening linkup with the airborne troops in the area of St. Mère Eglise.

The British landings had also been successful. Dempsey's II Army had advanced boldly toward Caen and were reported to have joined up with their airborne elements north of the city.

Omaha Beach, on the other hand, threatened disaster. Despite heroic efforts by the men of the 1st and 29th divisions, they had been unable to move off the beach and remained under heavy fire.

Bradley considered his options: While concentrated air attacks were hampering enemy efforts to reinforce the Omaha area, he knew that a German counterattack, even a weak one, could destroy the beachhead. He thought of evacuating the forces and diverting future waves to Utah and the British beaches. Considering the gravity of such a move, however, he decided to wait, praying that the men of Omaha could hold on until nightfall.

It was late afternoon when Rommel, hastily summoned from his brief holiday at Herrlingen, landed at the small airstrip close to his headquarters at La Roche Guyon.

In his office he studied the dismal reports.

While the 21st Panzer Division, racing for Caen, was even now engaging Montgomery's armor, no other significant movement of German reserves had been reported. The sleeping Führer, awakened at midafternoon, had grudgingly approved Von Runstedt's request for additional armored units. But Rommel knew they could not move until after sunset. The route to the beaches was lengthy and Allied air would take a terrible toll in daylight.

It would not take long. The Allied buildup would now be swift. Then a major breakout would see them sweep toward Germany. And what would he stop them with? Shattered units from the Russian front? Old men? Boys? If only he could have seen the Führer earlier, he thought, before the invasion. If only he could have convinced Hitler that armor close to the Channel was the only answer. If only.

Erwin Rommel brushed aside the damning reports and wearily rose to close the window against a sudden, chilling breeze. The rain had stopped. A light mist hung over the peaceful French village spread out below his castle headquarters. He thought of Lucie Maria and Manfred—and wished he were with them.

As June 6th neared its end, Allied fortunes continued to brighten. Bradley's decision not to evacuate Omaha Beach proved to be sound. By late afternoon, through the actions of men like Col. George A. Taylor of the 16th Infantry, the situation began to change. Taylor roamed the beach, urging his troops on while boldly exposing himself to enemy fire. "They're killing us here," he shouted. "Let's move inland and die there." One by one, they rose up to face the withering fire and followed the colonel inland. All across Omaha, incredibly brave men were showing the way.

As the sun settled over Normandy, the guns quieted. The Allied invaders, now 156,000 strong, paused to rest.

The Continent had been gained at the cost of 8,000 brave men. But the rest were there to stay.

At the Pas de Calais, the German XV Army, the one force that might have made the difference, also settled down for the night. Several miles across the Channel, strewn about the green fields of Kent, the soldierless barracks and empty tents—the wooden planes and rubber tanks of George Patton's fictitious army stood motionless in the deepening twilight.

P-38 Lightnings over France on D-Day—June 6, 1944.

The invasion fleet making a turn toward the beachhead.

Normandy, June 6, 1944. A Coast Guard pharmacist's mate gives aid to a wounded signalman aboard an LCI hit by a German 88 shell.

This signal bridge is on full alert during the Normandy invasion. This photograph was taken just prior to the landing aboard an LCI (Landing Craft, Infantry) on June 6.

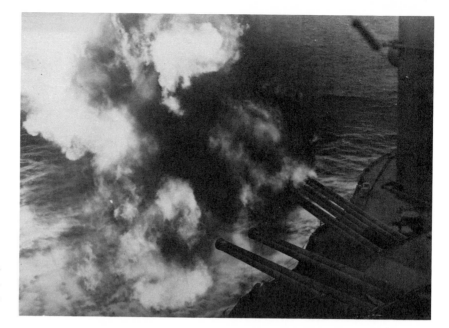

A heavy naval barrage softens up Utah Beach, where the first wave of infantry will soon hit the beach under machine-gun and mortar fire.

Fully equipped assault troops move through the surf on Utah Beach. June 7, 1944.

Utah Beach, June 7, 1944. Nazi 88mm shells explode on the beach as GI's try to move up to their next objective.

Normandy, June 8, 1944. An American tank moves down the ramp of an LST guided by one of the crew and the British Beachmaster.

Normandy, June 9, 1944. 8th Infantry Regiment troops of the 4th Division moving into a village after taking it from the Germans.

Normandy, June 9, 1944. Smoke pours out of German defenses after heavy shelling. Assault troops prepare to land. The shoulder patch shows they are a 1st Division unit.

Utah Beach. German 88mm shells explode alongside an LST as LCVPs head for the beach. June 12, 1944.

"Fox Green" landing area, June 12, 1944. The 5th Engineers, Special Brigade, land on the northern coast of France.

Normandy, June 12, 1944. Long lines of men and materiel stream ashore. This ever increasing flow of troops and equipment would support advance units.

Normandy, June 12, 1944. 5th Rangers of the 116th Regimental Combat team at a command post on the cliffs. The American flag is flown to protect them from fire from our own forces. Captured Germans are being led away.

June 12, 1944. French civilians welcome three American soldiers. Left to right: Pvt. Clem Lore, of Caldwell, Ohio; Sgt. Vincent de Angelis, Providence, R.I.; and Pvt. Robert Ryan, Schenectady, N.Y. The photograph was taken in the village of St. Honorine, June 12, 1944.

Utah Beach, June 12, 1944. 1st Lt. Morris W. Self, from Bear Lake, Michigan; Pfc. James Stanton, of Pauling, N.Y.; and 2nd Lt. Walter Sidowski, of Brooklyn, change into dry clothes after rescuing eight GI's from an LCVP that sank.

June 13, 1944. Barrage balloons prevent low-flying German fighter aircraft from strafing the ships.

Carantan, June 14, 1944. Paratrooper patrol passes dead soldiers hit by German sniper fire.

Cherbourg, June 28, 1944. American GI's take cover after placing an explosive charge against a Nazi pillbox.

June 28, 1944. The 313th Infantry of the 79th Division shepherd a long line of German prisoners toward a rear-area stockade.

July 1, 1944. Ships offshore waiting for transport to receive supplies to support the front line units moving forward.

July 7, 1944. The French Arsenal at the Passin Napoleon II is blasted into ruins. It was a base for German "E" motor torpedo boats.

July 20, 1944. An advance guard of the 29th Infantry Regiment enters shambles that was St. Lo.

St. Lo, July 22, 1944. French civilians watch (left background) as German prisoners guarded by a tank are processed for prisoner-of-war camps.

CHAPTER 5 PURSUIT TO THE RHINE

"This unequal struggle is inevitably drawing to a close."

—Erwin Rommel's last letter to Adolf Hitler.

Dawn broke full and clear over the dew-soaked apple orchard housing the field headquarters of the U.S. I Army in France.

In his command tent, Gen. Omar Bradley sat hunched over a table strewn with papers. He had already been awake for hours, fine tuning his Operation Cobra, a major First Army effort to break out of the Normandy area. The day, July 25, 1944, promised to be one of the most critical of the war.

As he awaited word that Cobra had been launched, Bradley's restless mind pored over the 49 days of trial and sacrifice endured by the Allied armies since the D-Day landings. He was startled to find he could recall each of them with surprising clarity.

After securing the beachhead and broadening the lodgment area, his First Army advance had bogged down in Normandy's bocage country, an area covered by miles of rectangular farmland patches, each of them surrounded by thick hedges and deep ditches. In assaulting these hedgerows, American tanks found their undersides vulnerable to German antitank fire. Gen. Hauser's VII Army, opposing the advance, had taken full advantage of this difficult terrain. American casualties had been heavy. One of Bradley's generals, a veteran of the Guadalcanal fighting, had likened the bocage fighting to jungle combat against the Japanese.

The Allies' next major concern had been the capture of Cherbourg, a port located at the northern end of the Cotentin Peninsula. While artificial docks—known as Mulberries—had been successfully handling the essential supplies flowing to the British and American beaches, a major port facility was desperately needed.

In mid-June, Bradley had sent his 7th Corps in a rapid sweep across the base of the Cotentin, isolating the peninsula. Thousands of Hauser's weary troops scurried northward toward Cherbourg. The Americans placed the port under siege.

But Hitler, determined to deny the Allies its facilities, had ordered a "last man" resistance. Bloody fighting preceded Cherbourg's surrender on June 26th.

Southward advances had taken Bradley's I Army through the hedgerows to St. Lo on July 20th. It was from there that Cobra was being launched.

While the American advance in the west had been slow but steady, Montgomery's forces had remained hopelessly stalled north of Caen. It was there, where the Allies held positions closest to Germany, that Hitler most feared a breakout. Accordingly, he had concentrated huge masses of armor before Gen. Dempsey's British II Army, denying them Caen until July 22nd.

The seven weeks since Normandy beach had seen other significant developments in the European war.

Hitler's surprising dismissal of Field Marshal Gerd von Runstedt, Germany's veteran commander of the west, had been followed by the serious wounding of Erwin Rommel in a strafing attack.

Then, on July 20th, the Allied camp had been stunned to learn of the attempt on Hitler's life by high officers in his military—further evidence of a growing rebellion within the German High Command over the Führer's conduct of the war.

Bradley had long been convinced that Hitler was Germany's greatest enemy. His insistence on a yard-by-yard defense of the Normandy battleground—a strategy that had cost him dearly—only confirmed this. Hitler's badly mauled armies were now dangerously understrength. The time was right for a massive Allied breakout. Cobra, a planned four-corps sweep to the south and east, was intended to do just that.

An earlier breakout attempt by the I Army had ended in failure as had an effort by Montgomery at Caen. Fears were being expressed in the press that a stalemate reminiscent of World War I was in the offing. Cobra simply had to work.

Tensely awaiting word of the attack, Bradley reviewed the plan. Following an opening air strike, Gen. Collins's 7th Corps was to move out of St. Lo and dash southwest for Coutances. Troy Middleton's 8th Corps would attack on his right. When a breakthrough occurred, Bradley was prepared to push his armor through the breach.

For most of the morning, the I Army commander remained in his tent, reviewing initial reports of the attack. The air strike had stunned the German units facing Collins. American forces had pushed through the breach and were on the move.

By late afternoon, after a tense day, Bradley felt confident that Collins was on his way. The German 84th Corps was falling back. The breakthrough had been accomplished.

On the following day, July 26th, Collins's 7th Corps took Marigny and the U.S. 2nd and 3rd Armored Divisions poured through the hole to exploit the situation. Middleton's 8th Corps also drove southward. On the 28th, when his 4th Armored Division rolled into Coutance, the initial goals of Cobra had been achieved.

The I Army's slashing advance was more than Bradley could have hoped for. Buoyed by the news, he committed his 5th and 19th corps to the battle, urging his commanders to press on with all speed.

On July 31st, the 6th Armored Division of 8th Corps entered Avranches, 35 miles south of St. Lo, while the 4th Armored pushed on toward the opening to the port-rich Brittany Peninsula.

Everywhere, the Germans fell back in disorder. Field Marshal Guenther von Kluge, who had taken over for the dismissed Von Runstedt, received an urgent message from his field commander. "The entire left flank has collapsed," it read.

Patton, recently arrived in France to take command of the newly organized U.S. III Army, wrote Eisenhower: "My fear is that Bradley will win the war before I can get into it."

On August 1, 1944, Patton's III Army was officially activated. Its first assignment—to move into the Brittany Peninsula and capture its valuable ports.

On that same day, Omar Bradley took over as commander of the newly formed XII Army Group, consisting of Patton's III Army and Bradley's former command, the U.S. I, headed by Maj. Gen. Courtney Hodges. Bradley now led more than 400,000 American troops.

George Patton lost no time in getting his III Army on the move. When his 4th Armored Division reached the Selune River to find the bridge at Pontaubault intact, Patton said, "All through military history, wars have been lost because bridges weren't crossed." He ordered Troy Middleton's 8th Corps, now part of the III Army, over the bridge in pursuit of the German XXV, a jumble of units, many leaderless, fleeing toward the Brittany ports of St. Malo, Brest, Lorient, and St. Nazaire. The remainder of Patton's forces prepared to join Hodges's I Army in a two-army push toward the east.

On August 6th, at OB West headquarters, Field Marshal von Kluge listened patiently as an apoplectic Adolf Hitler made impossible demands at the other end of the telephone.

Although reeling from the force of Allied ground and air attacks against his positions, the field marshal had been planning a limited counteroffensive against Mortain, a weak point in the Allied line. It was designed to throw the Allied advance off stride and facilitate a German withdrawal toward the Seine.

But the Führer now insisted upon a major action aimed at cutting between the I and III armies, isolating Patton in Brittany, then driving to the Channel. Promising reinforcements, he called the action "a decisive blow."

These were the ravings of a sick man, Von Kluge knew. But he feared that Hitler might be aware of his association with those who had plotted the failed assassination. Choosing to cooperate, he agreed to launch the attack. The Führer's reinforcements, he said, were free to exploit any gains he achieved.

Von Kluge's counterattack got underway on August 7th. Through clever maneuvering, Bradley shored up the weak points in his line. Although Mortain fell, Maj. Gen. Leland Hobb's 30th Division stopped the German panzers nine miles short of Avranches. On August 10th, Von Kluge began a gradual withdrawal to the east.

In Brittany Patton's III Army continued its assault. On August 12th Nantes fell. Five days later, the port of St. Malo surrendered to the 83rd Division after a stubborn defense. Brest would resist until mid-September. The bypassed garrisons at St. Nazaire and Lorient would hold out until the end of the war.

At the same time, the Allied armies continued hammering eastward, toward Argentan and Le Mans, with Hodges's I Army advancing on the left and Patton's III on the right.

At about this time, the launching of a new offensive by Montgomery gave birth to a daring plan by Omar Bradley. Bradley discussed it with Patton, then with Eisenhower. Both men endorsed it enthusiastically.

With the Canadian I Army moving southward, toward Falaise, Bradley proposed turning his own 15th Corps north at Le Mans for a rapid advance to Argentan. When the Canadians took Falaise, they would press on to link up with the Americans, thereby encircling the entire German army in Normandy. Von Kluge, weakened by his failed Mortain offensive, would hardly have the strength to fight his way out of the tightly sealed pocket. In the ensuing massacre, Bradley predicted, the German V and VII armies would be annihilated.

It was a once-in-a-lifetime opportunity that could shorten the European war by months. With Eisenhower's blessings, Bradley set the plan in motion.

As his 15th Corps pushed northward, Bradley realized that the Canadian advance toward Falaise was proceeding at a disappointingly slow pace. Once again, Montgomery's forces were being severely criticized for what was perceived as a "timid advance."

With Von Kluge desperately maneuvering to avoid disaster, the 15th Corps raced into Argentan. But the Canadians had yet to take Falaise. The trap had not been closed.

Patton, ever impatient, ordered Gen. Haislip, commander of the 15th, to push on toward Falaise, a clear violation of Allied boundary agreements with the British. Bradley, anxious to avoid open war with the fussy Montgomery, ordered Patton to pull Haislip back to Argentan. A petulant Patton complied.

It was not until August 17th that Falaise fell. By that time, thousands of Von Kluge's troops had already slipped through the narrow escape corridor and fled eastward. What might have been the coup de grace for Hitler's armies in the west had proved to be something quite less.

Two days later, when Canadian and American units linked up farther east, at Chambois, the Falaise pocket was finally sealed. Inside the deadly circle, thousands of Von Kluge's soldiers were slaughtered by Allied artillery and air as they tried to escape. But the golden opportunity had passed. Even the vast number of German prisoners taken and equipment destroyed was little consolation for the distraught Bradley.

At his headquarters at St. Germaine en Laye, the disgraced Von Kluge, informed that he was to be replaced by Field Marshal Walther Model, was ordered to return to Germany immediately.

With his part in the July assassination plot undoubtedly revealed, the wretched Von Kluge knew that only trial and death awaited him. On his return, he stopped at Metz to draft a final note in which he begged Hitler to seek peace. "The German people have suffered unspeakable ills," he wrote. "The time has come to put an end to these horrors."

After making sure of the letter's prompt delivery, Von Kluge, architect of so many German victories, ended his life by swallowing potassium cyanide.

The Falaise Gap concluded the battle of Normandy. Having suffered more than a half-million casualties since D-Day, the bloodied German army now streamed eastward toward the Seine.

On the Mediterranean coast, 60,000 men of Gen. Alexander Patch's U.S. VII Army stormed ashore on August 15th, launching Operation Anvil, an invasion of southern France.

While French units under Gen. Jean de Lattre de Tassigny moved westward to capture the ports of Toulon and Marseilles, Patch's forces began a northward advance up the valley of the Rhone aimed at an eventual linkup with Patton's Third Army.

The irrepressible Patton continued to roar across France. "Old Blood and Guts" as he was now known, pearl-handled pistols at his sides, led his armored units in a mad dash for the Seine. On his left, Hodges's I Army struggled to keep pace.

With his forces closing on Paris, Eisenhower now faced a difficult decision. His original intention had been to bypass the French capital, cross the Seine, then continue a hot pursuit of the enemy toward the German frontier. But other developments intervened.

With Patton's 15th Corps already across the river at Mantes-Gassicourt, only 30 miles northwest of Paris, resistance elements inside the city, sensing imminent liberation, rose up against their German captors. The French capital was soon in turmoil.

Gen. Charles de Gaulle, leader of the Free French Movement and newly arrived from North Africa, pleaded with Eisenhower to occupy Paris before a bloodbath occurred. Privately, De Gaulle feared that a Communist-led French government would seize control of the city before his entry.

While reluctant to interrupt his pursuit of the German army, Eisenhower relented, ordering Gen. Henri le Clerc's French 2nd Armored Division to race for the capital. Ray Barton's battle-hardened 4th Division was sent to assist.

On August 25th, Le Clerc's armor rolled into Paris and, amidst wild celebrations, accepted the surrender of the German commander, Gen. Dietrich von Cholitz, who had boldly defied Hitler's order to burn the city.

With Eisenhower's armies now across the Seine both north and south of Paris, a plan advanced by Gen. Montgomery created sharp divisions within the Allied camp.

Monty proposed abandoning the "two thrust" strategy for operations beyond the Seine—namely a British advance to the northeast while American forces struck east and southeast—in favor of a "single thrust" of four Allied armies, all under his command. His plan called for a rapid advance toward the Pas de Calais and the destruction of the German XV Army. After taking Antwerp and Rotterdam—destroying en route the launching sites of the V1 and V2 aerial bombs that were ravaging London—Monty proposed a bold sweep through the industrial Ruhr to Berlin.

Although the original plan of Overlord called for Eisenhower to assume ground control of all Allied troops in Europe as soon as the breakout from Normandy had been achieved, it was widely known that Montgomery sought to retain that control for himself. His latest plan was seen as a blatant attempt to strike out boldly with 40 English and American divisions, reaping the personal glory of victory, while Patton's III Army sat impotently behind and Bradley, the XII Army Group commander, was left with little to command.

Eisenhower found himself in the middle of a raging controversy that gravely threatened Anglo-American harmony. In the end, he compromised, giving Montgomery "operating coordination" of Hodges's I Army as it joined his XXI Army Group's northeastward thrust. Patton's two-corps army—his VIII was still regrouping after operations in Brittany—would continue to fight on Hodges's right.

Beginning on August 26th, the Allied front moved out to the east and northeast. Both Montgomery and Patton made rapid advances.

While Crerar's Canadian I Army moved toward Boulogne and Calais, Dempsey's II Army pressed for the Belgian border.

As Patton drove toward Nancy and Metz, his armor rolled through the historic battlefields of World War I—St. Mihiel, Rheims, Verdun. By September 1st, his 12th and 20th corps had established beachheads across the Meuse River, just 60 miles from the German border.

Montgomery's XXI Army Group continued its own advance with no less electrifying results. Crossing into Belgium, the

British 30th Corps took Brussels on September 3rd and Antwerp two days later. But there, with the Rhine at Arnhem only 75 miles away, the always-cautious Montgomery chose to stop. Monty had another master plan to sell.

With Allied supply lines lengthening, necessitating the hauling of supplies by truck over a 700-mile route from the Normandy beachheads and Cherbourg, Eisenhower was anxious to get the port at Antwerp into operation as soon as possible. But the Germans still controlled the outlying Scheldt Estuary, which effectively denied Antwerp's facilities to the Allies.

Ike pressed Montgomery to reduce the Walcherens Islands, commanding the estuary, and get the port in operation. But Monty had another scheme in mind.

It was called "Market Garden," a daring and imaginative strike into Holland in which the Anglo-American I Airborne Army would be dropped at several points along the road to Arnhem. While the paratroopers seized vital road junctions and river crossings, Miles Dempsey's II Army would make a lightning thrust from the area of the Albert Canal, join up with the paratroopers along the way and capture Arnhem. After its fall, Monty said, he would initiate his war-ending thrust through the Ruhr to Berlin.

Eisenhower was intrigued by the notion of a bridgehead across the Rhine at Arnhem. But the plan was fraught with problems and the Antwerp problem needed immediate attention.

Despite the objections of Bradley and others—who feared that the Germans were reorganizing at the German border for a fierce defense of the *Vaterland*—Ike approved the plan. But he turned down Montgomery's proposed advance into the Ruhr should the mission succeed.

With ominous warnings from Allied intelligence that strong panzer units had been moved to the Arnhem area, Montgomery launched Market Garden. In the face of fierce German resistance, it failed—at the cost of 17,000 Allied soldiers killed, wounded, or missing.

The resulting delay in Allied operations necessitated a long and difficult campaign to clear the Scheldt Estuary and open Antwerp to Allied shipping. It was not until late November that supplies began to trickle through the Belgian port.

During the long advance from southern France, Gen. Patch's U.S. VII Army had been joined by the French First, commanded by Gen. de Lattre. Together, they were formed into the Sixth Army Group, under the command of Lt. Gen. Jacob Devers.

On September 11th, when Patch's forces, advancing northward, made contact with the right of Patton's III Army, the Allies held a continuous line from Switzerland to the North Sea.

On that same day, patrols of the U.S. I Army crossed the German frontier, near Aachen. Not since the days of Napoleon had Germany been invaded from the west.

Aachen, the ancient imperial city known for its art treasures, was placed under siege. Realizing that its loss would open the way to the Rhine, the Germans fought furiously. When the historic place capitulated a month later, it lay in ruins.

East of Aachen, operations commenced in the densely wooded Huertgen Forest. Once again, I Army forces found themselves locked in a deadly struggle with a stubborn enemy. Fighting in the cold and rain, American units suffered disastrous losses before the forest was cleared of German troops.

With Eisenhower determined to keep constant pressure on the reeling German army, November 1944 brought a general offensive all along the Allied line.

In the north, Simpson's IX Army, now positioned between Dempsey's II and Hodges's I, joined forces with the British in bloody village-by-village combat against an enemy determined to hold the Netherlands line.

In the center, while Hodges's I Army continued pounding at the enemy's Siegfried defenses, Patton's III launched a major offensive toward the Saar.

In the south, Patch's VII Army initiated operations in the area of the Belfort Gap designed to close the escape corridor for German troops fleeing northward. At the same time, the French I Army moved through the Vosges mountains, toward the Rhine plain.

Heavy rain slowed the advance. But Eisenhower pushed on, determined to reach the Rhine before the onset of winter. He was not to be denied.

At 6:30 P.M. on November 19, 1944, a detachment of the French I Army, fighting near the Swiss border, suddenly broke into the Rhine plain and sighted the river at a place called Rosenau.

The long pursuit that had begun at St. Lo almost four months before was over. The fierce, final battle of Germany was about to begin.

June 16, 1944. The 15th Air Force hits the oil refineries at Loban, Austria.

Arles, France, June 21, 1944. Bombs from Allied bombers destroy the Nazi retreat bridge across the Rhone River.

Cannisy, France, July 27, 1944. An armored vehicle passes houses hit by U.S. shellfire. Accurate artillery barrages helped drive the Germans out.

St. Lo, July 29, 1944. Jeeps drive through the devastated town.

July 31, 1944. An M-4 tank knocked out in the attack on Avranches.

Percy, France, August 2, 1944. 109th Regiment of the 28th Infantry Division is looking for snipers. A BAR man covers as his buddies start "housecleaning."

Tessy-sur-Vire, August 3, 1944. American troops and armor occupy the town. German units are still holed up in the buildings.

August 3, 1944. An American tank under attack as it enters the village of St. Sever Calvados.

August 8, 1944. British and American troops have taken Vire. A patrol checks the street for snipers. The city was under German mortar fire from the surrounding hills.

Coudrey, August 8, 1944. Tanks and infantry concentrate on wiping out a German machine-gun nest just off the Coudrey road.

115th Infantry of the 29th Infantry Division march through Vire toward the enemy. They have just been in a heavy firefight in taking the town on August 9, 1944.

August 1944. Five 8th Air Force P-47's caught this German troop train rounding a curve at a town named Gisers.

Woelfing, August 10, 1944. Troops of the 44th Infantry Division in search of German snipers. Soldiers cover the moving GI's. The German soldier was hit by covering fire.

August 12, 1944. 314th Infantry of the 79th Division leaving Mamers. It was just a short walk to the next fight.

Ste. Maxine, southern France, August 15, 1944. Infantry of the 45th Division leave their LCI's and wade ashore in hip-deep water.

August 15, 1944. LCI's and LVCP's land troops on the beaches of St. Tropez.

The first troops on the beach, August 15, 1944. They are engineers blowing lanes through the minefield with "Bangalore Torpedoes."

GI's moving inland. August 15, 1944.

A 12-foot wall affords cover for this squad, which has come under heavy fire from a German machine-gun emplacement.

Dinard, France, August 16, 1944. The VII Army and Free French forces aboard as the invasion force approaches the coast of southern France.

A BAR (Browning Automatic Rifle) man fires into the underbrush before moving forward with his unit. August 17, 1944.

Flassan, southern France. An American M-4 tank hit by German 88mm shells burns at the side of the road. August 17, 1944.

Somewhere in France, August 17, 1944. The 5th Ranger Battalion communications center. T/4 Norman C. Seeley (writing); Pfc. Loouyie Riava (holding rifle) from Danville, Ill.; and Pvt. Henry Picksrz (driving) from Newburgh, N.Y.

Danielle, August 21, 1944. The line of retreat
of German units is pointed out by a French
civilian. The GI's are from the 41st Regiment
of the 2nd Armored Division.

Fontainebleau, August 23, 1944. A U.S. tank
moves forward as infantry fires at the Germans across the Seine River.

Paris, August 25, 1944. The city is plagued
by lingering rearguard actions. American and
particularly French forces fight for the liberation of Paris.

Paris, August 26, 1944. A woman takes refuge from German sniper fire—a delaying tactic to provide a breathing spell for the withdrawal of Nazi forces.

Allied aircraft bomb German headquarters in Paris on August 26, 1944.

Paris, August 26, 1944. German sniper fire from a building on the Place de la Concorde scatters citizens to take cover. Although the Germans had surrendered Paris, small bands of snipers still remained.

Paris, August 26, 1944. Scenes like this were common in Paris as snipers and collaborators were rounded up after the city's liberation. The man in the center of the picture, with blood streaming down his face, has been beaten by irate citizens, and has been arrested by police, who are taking him away.

Paris, August 26, 1944. A partial view of the crowd in the Place de la Concorde as a liberation parade passes by.

Paris, August 26, 1944. The crowd at the Arc de Triomphe as circling aircraft dip their wings in a salute to the liberators.

Paris, August 27, 1944. The Ecole de Tonn-
ellerie is in smoky ruins.

Marseilles, southern France, August 28,
1944. The Basilica of Notre Dame de la Garde
comes under Nazi artillery fire.

Paris, August 29, 1944. The 28th Division
marched down the Champs Elysées to the
Arc de Triomphe. After this brief and moving
interlude, the 28th immediately returned to
the front line.

Here the 29th Infantry Division nears the Arc de Triomphe, August 29, 1944.

The Franco-Belgian border, September 2, 1944. A column of U.S. 6 x 6 trucks pass a sign marking the Belgian frontier.

The Meuse River, September 5, 1944, near Roux, Belgium. U.S. infantry run across a footbridge under fire.

Belgium, September 6, 1944. An American armored car looks for German resistance among the burning ruins.

Dinant, Belgium, September 7, 1944. The 9th Infantry Division engineers float a pontoon section out. It will hook with pontoons on the far shore. These men are from the 15th Engineer Battalion.

Rigney, southern France, September 9, 1944.
A 3rd Division 81mm mortar squad fires on
German positions.

Chartres, France, September 1944. Beneath
the smoke and flames is what remains of a
German "Tiger" tank.

Meuse River, Belgium, September 11, 1944.
At Argenteau, Belgians of "The White Army"
ferry U.S. infantrymen across the river.

Belgium, September 1944. French troops guard German prisoners.

Bayon, France, September 12, 1944. U.S. Army medics at work in the fury of tank warfare. A medic runs in front of a flaming tank as its ammunition explodes. Another medic attends to a wounded soldier.

September 12, 1944. 1st Division troops move on the road leading to Aachen, the first German city in more than a century to be attacked by an enemy.

Aachen, September 14, 1944. 1st Division GI's run past a burning half-track hit by German fire.

Meuse River, Holland, September 14, 1944. At Maastricht, Dutch rowboats and assault boats ferry men of H Company, 117th Infantry, of the 30th Infantry Division across the river.

Aachen, September 15, 1944. Sniper fire pins down soldiers caught in the open.

Aachen, September 15, 1944. A dead German soldier lies amid ruins of the ancient city.

September 19, 1944. The 103rd Engineers of the 28th Division demolished this pillbox. The blast threw the heavy door 200 feet away.

Aachen. Troops of the 1st Division try to flush out German snipers.

Muerth River, France, September 22, 1944. The 314th Infantry of the 9th Division take heavy casualties from German fire from the far bank. The unit is being supported by tank fire.

Verdun, France, October 1, 1944. Lt. Margaret White, Morristown, Pa.; Lt. Ellen Ludwig, South Williamsport, Pa.; and Capt. Edalia S. Ruciniski, of Garner, Mass., look at an electric iron found in the ruins of Verdun.

Bruyères, France. A team of Japanese-American GI's fire 105mm shells at Germans in support of an American infantry attack. October 18, 1944.

Bruyères, October 24, 1944. Japanese-American infantrymen moving up a hillside toward German positions.

October 29, 1944. Advance aid station manned by medics. There is a lull. Soon the casualties will fill the stretchers, and most will be sent down to clearing stations on their way to evacuation hospitals and general hospitals. This aid station is at Beemont, France.

Manhoue, France, November 9, 1944. Armored vehicles of the 3rd Armored Division crowd the streets of the town, which is just north of Nancy. They are moving up to the front.

Metz, France. GI's of the 1st Battalion of the 378th Infantry of the 95th Division move into the center of Metz during heavy fighting. November 17, 1944.

95th Infantry patrol a section of Metz on November 20, 1944. They are looking for snipers.

Metz. German officers surrender Fort Jeanne D'Arc, the last fort to fall. The Germans surrendered when they ran out of ammunition. The captors are from the 101st Infantry Regiment of the 26th Infantry Division.

Zweifall, Germany, November 24, 1944. A Sherman tank with a flamethrower attacks German positions.

Gueberling, France. Units of the 26th Infantry Division knocked out three German Panther tanks in heavy combat on November 24–25, 1944.

November 25, 1944. GI's of the 318th Infantry of the 80th Infantry Division capture German soldiers hiding in a Maginot Line fort near St. Avold.

Puttelange, December 4, 1944. The 134th Regiment of the 35th Infantry Division moving through an open field in pursuit of Germans. The buildings have been repeatedly hit by artillery fire.

Grandvilliers, France, December 4, 1944.
Company C of the 83rd Chemical Battalion,
45th Division, fires a 4.2 mortar on enemy
troops in the woods.

Bischweiler, France, December 8, 1944. The
313 Infantry Regiment, 79th Division, de-
ploys along a road on the alert for heavy
sniper fire. The 7th Army troops have fought
north from the sunny coast of southern
France. Despite heavy fighting all the way, it
was known among the units that remained in
Italy as "The Champagne Campaign." The
phrase originated with war cartoonist Bill
Mauldin.

Niederbron, France, December 10, 1944. A
tense moment during a sniper hunt. The
infantryman on the right is going to open the
door. His two buddies are ready to fire.

December 13, 1944. The 92nd Cavalry Recon Squad of the 12th Armored Division in preparation for an attack. An old and obsolete Maginot Line pillbox is used as a shield to observe enemy activity.

December 31, 1944. The 357th Infantry fires a new type of white phosphorous Bazooka shell against the wall of a Maginot Line fort.

Bertring, France, January 19, 1945. An 11th Corps, 7th Army fuel truck explodes after being hit by enemy fire.

Pit Wingen, France, March 18, 1945. Company K, 3rd Battalion, 1093 Division, moves up a slope into rolling country near the eastern German border.

CHAPTER 6 THE BATTLE OF THE BULGE

"This is surely the Führer's final madness."

—A Wermacht general when told of Hitler's Ardennes plan.

It was early December 1944 and the icy mantle of winter had descended upon the western front. Since the July breakout at St. Lo, the Allied armies had raged across France in pursuit of the fleeing *Wehrmacht*. Hermann Göring's Luftwaffe lay mortally wounded. Allied bombers were pounding German industry day and night. Even the most optimistic of Hitler's generals had long since abandoned any hope of victory. Some quietly sought avenues for peace.

Now, with his troops pressing toward the Rhine, General Eisenhower paused to plan the final campaign of the European war, the battle for Germany.

Allied spirits were soaring. Their forces now held a 500-mile line running from Switzerland to the North Sea.

November offensives saw the British and Canadians continue their advance through the Low Countries.

Below them, in the American I Army sector, the Siegfried Line had been breached at several points.

In the south, with some units of the French First Army already camped on the west bank of the Rhine, George Patton pressed his III Army attacks toward the Saar.

Everywhere, the scent of victory was in the air. The war in Europe, it was said, would be over in a few months.

But Eisenhower had one major concern: As British and Canadian forces struggled to open the port of Antwerp, materiel for his 54 Allied divisions in the line had to be trucked more than 500 miles from Cherbourg and the Normandy beaches. With supply lines stretched perilously thin, there was a constant shortage of troops and ammunition.

But Eisenhower knew that an extended delay in the Allied advance would give the Germans time to recover from their long retreat. Determined to keep pressure on his resilient enemy, he ordered the American I and IX, part of Omar Bradley's XII Army Group, to launch a major offensive toward the Ruhr, center of Germany's industrial might.

With troops in short supply, Bradley had to make concessions somewhere. In what he termed "a calculated risk," he stretched five American divisions across a broad 80-mile front in the Belgian Ardennes. Several of these units were newly arrived and untested in battle. The others, torn up in recent heavy fighting, were resting.

This same Ardennes front had been the scene of a costly breakthrough by the Germans in May 1940. In that attack, as the French line crumbled, the Führer's armor had streamed westward, toward Paris. Within a month, France was out of the war.

While Allied intelligence had noted recent enemy troop movements in the area, they had convinced Eisenhower that Hitler was no longer capable of waging a major offensive. Beyond that, they reasoned, the Germans were unlikely to attack in the same area as the 1940 offensive. As a consequence, Eisenhower accepted the reasoning and the risk.

Plagued by thoughts of a new Russian offensive in the Danube Valley and fears that the Allies were about to launch a major effort into Germany, Hitler was determined to make one last bid to change the course of the war. Surprisingly, he chose to strike again through the Ardennes and drive on to Antwerp and Brussels. By splitting the British and American armies and cutting them off from their supplies, he hoped to force separate peace negotiations with the western Allies. He was then free to shift the full weight of his military to the Russian front.

It was a bold and ambitious plan, one with little chance of success. But Hitler was not to be denied. Despite strong objections from his generals, most of whom he no longer trusted since the failed July attempt on his life, he set about gathering three great armies inside a forest preserve facing the Ardennes, a place known as the Schnee Eifel.

Gerd von Runstedt was recalled from retirement to serve as nominal head of the campaign. The 70-year-old field marshal, ill and disillusioned by the course of the war, argued that the plan was far beyond the strength of the battered German army. But Hitler brushed aside his objections.

With any hope for success dependent upon secrecy and surprise, the assault force began assembling behind the fog and mist blanketing the Schnee Eifel. German units, many recalled from the Russian sector, moved only in darkness. Allied troops were puzzled by the nightly appearance of low-flying Luftwaffe fighters buzzing the front. In fact, they were shielding the sound of German armor moving into position. In this manner, three armies comprising more than 250,000 men were put into place by mid-December. H-hour, twice postponed, was set for 0530, December 16, 1944.

Hitler's battle plan was revealed to the frontline commanders only hours before the attack. It provided that the VI Panzer Army, under newly promoted Col. Gen. Sepp Dietrich, attack in the north at Monschau, thrust northwest for the Meuse River, capturing Liège, then drive for Antwerp. Dietrich's army was made up largely of SS troops, fanatical, battle-toughened young men who were crazed with patriotism.

At the center, Baron Hasso von Manteuffel's Fifth Panzer Army was to dash for the Meuse, cross between Namur and Dinant, then close on Brussels.

In the south, the VII Army, commanded by General Erich Brandenberger, was ordered to provide flank protection for the entire operation.

In the early hours of December 16th, the last of Hitler's armor rumbled into place. At III Army headquarters near the Saar, Gen. Patton noted with unease the radio stillness along the entire western front. Prophetically, he asked that an immediate plan be drawn up should his forces be called upon to attack northward.

In the frozen Ardennes, the 80,000 American troops defending the front slumbered in their tents and foxholes. For most, it would be their last undisturbed rest for weeks. Some would soon be blasted awake to face the final day of their lives.

The battle began with a deafening roar as 2,000 guns opened up all along the 80-mile front. When the barrage lifted, white-shrouded German infantry moved out of the Schnee Eifel's snow and mist. Behind them, engines idling, the huge tanks waited to exploit the first breakthrough.

Hitler's 12 infantry and 9 panzer divisions, designated as Army Group B, smashed into the nine American infantry regiments defending the line. The power of the German attack was staggering. As their forces fell upon the weakly defended American positions, the Ardennes line sagged, then gave way. Surprised, frightened GI's fell back in dismay. Within hours, penetrations, some deep, were reported all along the line.

With communications knocked out by the fury of the attack, units adjacent to the Ardennes were unaware that a violent German offensive had begun. It was early afternoon before the attack was considered anything but a local action with limited goals.

Gen. Manteuffel's V Army roared through the center, overwhelming the green 106th Infantry Division defending the St. Vith road. Two of its regiments were quickly surrounded. Seven thousand Americans were forced to surrender.

In the south, leading elements of Gen. Brandenberger's VII Army crossed the Our River, then pushed on to Wiltz, 12 miles to the west. There, they were temporarily halted by units of the American 8th Corps.

Only in the north was quick success denied, when Sepp Dietrich's 6th Panzers ran into a wall of resistance at Monschau. There, the U.S. 2nd and 99th, southernmost units of the 5th Corps, refused to budge. As their positions were pounded, the 2nd and 99th abandoned Monschau and retired to a natural defense line known as Elsenborn Ridge. Repelling repeated German attacks, they held tenaciously, denying Dietrich access to the vital Liège road. For the moment, the northern shoulder of the Allied line was secure.

By late afternoon of the 16th, the front was in chaos. Roving bands of German paratroops under Col. Friedrich von der Hyte were creating havoc behind the lines. In addition, a special commando force, led by Col. Otto Skorzeny, the fearless officer who had rescued Mussolini from Italian partisans in a daring 1943 raid, roamed about the rear, causing confusion and panic. Dressed in GI uniforms, driving American jeeps, these English-speaking infiltrators blew up bridges, changed road signs and spread alarmist rumors. Once their presence became known, emergency measures were quickly taken. At gun point, American GI's confronted each other, demanding to know who was married to Betty Grable or what football player lined up between the center and tackle. When Gen. Bradley correctly identified Springfield as the capital of Illinois, he had a few tense moments when his young interrogator insisted that the answer was Chicago. Recognized by others, the American commander was allowed to move on.

As the first day of battle drew to a close, the German advance continued. In the south, a soft spot in the American line gave way toward Bastogne. At the center, Manteuffel's V Army spearpoint was driving on St. Vith. In the north, a German battle group, led by the infamous SS Col. Joachen Peiper, slipped between the 5th and 8th Corps and raced for Stavelot, deep in the American rear.

When the scope of the German offensive was at last recognized, Eisenhower and Bradley moved to reinforce the Ardennes front. From a rest area near Rheims, the 82nd and 101st Airborne divisions were motor convoyed, headlights blazing, toward Bastogne. The U.S. 7th Armored was ordered to speed for St. Vith. Eisenhower knew that a successful defense of these two road junctions was essential.

As night fell on the snow-covered Ardennes, the confused,

outnumbered Americans continued to give ground. From battle-field headquarters, Field Marshal von Runstedt joyously wired his Führer that a great German victory was at hand.

December 17th. As Allied intelligence officers pored over their maps in an attempt to assess the scope and intention of the German attack, the complexion of the conflict began to emerge.

The fabric of the battle was made up of countless small combats in key sectors. While reinforcements raced toward the front, scattered American units were engaged in many critical holding actions: A crossroad would be defended by a handful of men, a bridge blown up by the remnants of a platoon. In terrain that offered little opportunity for cross-country tank maneuver, small groups of Americans were denying Hitler's armor use of the Ardennes roads. Without question, the seeds of Germany's defeat were sown in those critical, heroic first hours.

It was soon clear that a great bulge had developed at the center of the American line. But vital points were holding. In the north, the U.S. 7th Armored Division outraced the Germans to St. Vith. Just hours after the 101st Airborne rolled into Bastogne, the town was surrounded by the enemy.

At the spearpoint of the German advance, the SS unit commanded by Col. Peiper captured a group of 7th Armored Division artillerymen in the area of Malmedy. Herded into a snowy field, the 125 Americans were ruthlessly gunned down. Only a handful survived to tell the gruesome story.

The German V Army had been stopped cold before St. Vith. In desperation, Gen. Manteuffel bypassed the city and drove for Spa, where vast supplies of fuel had been stored for use in the planned American offensive. Since most of the German units had started the attack with only a limited supply, capture of these frontline dumps was essential.

At Spa, Gen. Hodges quickly organized his First Army head-quarters staff for the town's defense and ordered the valuable fuel trucked to the rear.

On December 19th, with the equivalent of two Allied field armies en route to the front, Eisenhower, Bradley, and Patton met in emergency session at Verdun. Emphasizing that St. Vith and Bastogne must hold, Eisenhower ordered Patton to turn his III Army northward, toward the besieged Bastogne.

Recognizing that the bulge at the center of the line had cut off Bradley's XII Army Group headquarters from its northern troops, Eisenhower placed the I and IX armies under the command of Montgomery. The British commander was ordered to take up defensive positions along the Meuse to prevent a German cross-ing. Finally, plans were set in place for an Allied counteroffen-sive to begin as soon as the force of the Ardennes attack had been blunted.

December 20th. With the northern shoulder continuing to hold against Dietrich's VI and Brandenberger's VII armies stopped in the south, only the center of the Allied line continued to give way. There, Manteuffel's forces, having bypassed Bastogne, pressed their advance toward the Meuse.

On the 21st, anxious to form a coherent line of resistance rather than a scattered defense, Montgomery ordered the 7th Armored Division to abandon St. Vith. The American com-mander reluctantly obeyed. Jubilant at the news, Hitler renewed his demands that Bastogne must fall.

In that beleaguered place, attacks by the 24th Volksgrenadiers increased in their fury. With Patton's III Army fighting its way toward the city's relief, Bastogne's defenders continued to throw back every German assault.

Since the battle's beginning, snow and heavy fog had made Allied air support impossible. But daybreak on December 23rd brought blue skies. Planes of the U.S. 9th Air Force took off to pound the columns of German armor jamming all roads leading to the front. Flying more than 10,000 sorties during the next five days, the American airmen wreaked havoc behind the enemy lines, strafing supply trains, bombing troop concentrations, and destroying communications. This appearance of American air power spelled certain disaster for Hitler's Ardennes offensive.

As the weather broke, the leading edge of the German V Army approached the Meuse close to Dinant. Only the U.S. 2nd Armored Division, supported by the British 29th Brigade, stood in Manteuffel's way.

On Christmas Eve a great battle began. The fighting, frequently hand to hand, raged into Christmas Day. Finally, on the 26th, the British and Americans launched a fierce counterattack and Manteuffel's line crumbled. Lack of gasoline and failure to seize the American fuel dumps had finally brought the 10-day enemy advance to a halt—barely four miles from its Meuse River objective.

In the late afternoon of the 26th, with a new German attack imminent, tanks of Patton's 4th Armored Division fought their way into Bastogne. While it was a precarious connection at best, it signaled the city's relief.

Although the force of the German offensive seemed spent, Hitler refused every request for a general withdrawal. Instead, he demanded a firm policy of "no retreat."

The Allied armies now set about the task of blunting and narrowing the bulge, more than 60 miles at its deepest penetration and 50 miles wide at its base. With the U.S. IX Army attacking from the north and Patton's III pushing up from the south, the Germans found themselves being squeezed into an ever-narrowing corridor as they retreated eastward.

On January 3, 1945, Montgomery began an offensive on the northern flank, designed to restore the original Ardennes line. By the 9th, the bulge had been narrowed to nine miles and the retreating Germans were being shelled from both north and south. By January 13th the Allies had destroyed 20 of the 24 German divisions that had begun the attack. On the 16th, the U.S. I and III armies linked up at Houffalize. For the first time in a month, Bradley's XII Army Group forces were joined together.

On January 23rd St. Vith was recaptured and the fleeing Germans, their ranks a shambles and under constant attack by Allied air, broke for the safety of their Siegfried defenses. Within a week, the original line of December 16th had been reestablished.

The 44-day Battle of the Bulge remains the largest in the history of American arms. Six hundred thousand U.S. soldiers took part, three times the number that fought on *both* sides at Gettysburg. American casualties totaled more than 80,000 men. Germany lost 100,000 of her best soldiers. Vast amounts of materiel had been destroyed on both sides. But while American strength could be quickly restored, German losses were irreplaceable. The Hitlerian policy of "no retreat" had doomed his nation to certain defeat.

With Allied forces in swift pursuit, the battered, bloodied survivors of Germany's last offensive fled eastward. Behind them, in the snowy silence of a Belgian fir forest, the charred ruins of three Nazi armies bore mute testimony to Adolf Hitler's shattered dream.

December 16, 1944. U.S. antiaircraft unit on alert, based along the "dragon's teeth" of the Siegfried Line. These men are from the 531st AA Battalion of the 30th Division.

Vielsala, Belgium, December 23, 1944. A 7th Armored Division antitank gun covers the road and railway crossing in town.

December 26, 1944. The 101st Airborne units move into Bastogne to give relief to its defenders.

December 28, 1944. 4th Armored Infantry units bring relief to the besieged city of Bastogne.

December 31, 1944. Company G, 1st Battalion, 345th Infantry Regiment of the 87th Infantry Division on the lookout for snipers as they move through the village of Moire, Belgium.

Pont, Belgium, January 17, 1945. 30th Infantry Division troops crawl across open terrain to avoid enemy fire. These soldiers are from E Company, 3rd Battalion.

Morhet, Belgium. VIII Corps armored vehicles park on a snowy slope waiting for orders to advance, January 1945.

Hamm, Germany, January 5, 1945. 1st Battalion, 378th Regiment of the 95th Division. A patrol moves into the center of the newly captured town. The roadblock was left by the retreating Nazis.

Ardennes Forest, January 14, 1945. 3rd Armored Division patrol. Vapor trails are from bombers en route to Germany. The GI's use fir trees for cover.

L'Ourthe River, Belgium, January 16, 1945. 84th Division and 11th Armored Division patrol rendezvous close to the Bulge.

A German tank hit by shells from the 703rd Tank Destroyer Battalion of the 3rd Armored Division.

Lomre, Belgium. A farmhouse hit by German artillery fire. U.S. troops run for cover. January 16, 1945.

Bovigny, Belgium. 83rd Division infantrymen man a 57mm antitank gun.

CHAPTER 7 THE BATTLE OF GERMANY

"Shove everything you can across it, Courtney."

—Omar Bradley's order to General Hodges on learning that the bridge at Remagen had been captured.

Karl Timmerman was growing anxious. Like thousands of American GI's slogging across Europe in the early spring of 1945, he was eager to see the Rhine—that last natural barrier available to the retreating enemy. Beyond it, all of Germany lay open to invasion. The rest would be a piece of cake.

It was late on the morning of March 7th as the young lieutenant led his company, an advance detachment of the 9th Armored Division, through the dense, rain-soaked Schnee Eifel woods, 50 miles inside of Germany. According to his map, the town of Remagen, nestled on the west bank of the Rhine midway between Cologne and Coblenz, was less than a mile ahead.

As a lowly company commander in a very big war, Timmerman knew that his view of things was necessarily narrow. But one thing was certain. With every Rhine bridge reportedly blown up and a strong German buildup in progress along the eastern shore, a general Allied advance across the river was going to take time. Months maybe. But that didn't bother Karl. Just reaching the river, he felt, was a major step on the long road back to West Point, Nebraska.

Ten minutes later, Timmerman's company emerged from the woods to look down upon Remagen. Just beyond, the muddied Rhine looked somber and forbidding, nothing like the sparkling, gently flowing version he had fantasized. Still, there it was, wide and inviting.

Ordering his men to remain under cover, the lieutenant took one of his platoon leaders and eased forward for a better look.

From the top of a hill they observed little movement in the town. The only activity came from the railway bridge that linked Remagen with the river's eastern shore. Some German military vehicles and a line of civilians were moving slowly across.

Timmerman studied the scene through his field glasses. Something, he wasn't sure what, didn't seem right. Then, it hit him with a wallop. The bridge was still standing. The Germans hadn't blown it.

Keeping it under surveillance, Timmerman ordered a runner to the rear to report his incredible find.

Word of the discovery spread like wildfire. A senior officer of the combat command raced to the scene and a decision was quickly made. The town would be taken and, if possible, the bridge with it.

By early afternoon, Karl Timmerman's company, joined by several others, had moved down the hill and cleaned out most of Remagen. Now, cautiously, they approached the span known as the Ludendorff Bridge. Timmerman warily eyed the ominous dynamite charges strapped beneath the structure. Any moment, he knew, the Germans on the far side could set the whole thing off. Nebraska suddenly seemed very far away.

As additional men and tanks were moved forward, the bridge was shaken by a shattering explosion two-thirds of the way across. Incredibly, the span rose up, shuddered, then settled back into place. The German attempt to destroy it had failed.

Events developed quickly. While engineers sought to defuse the remaining charges, Timmerman's company was ordered onto the bridge. Gunshots erupted from the far side. A dozen separate firefights ensued. While the engineers labored feverishly in the face of the German fire, Timmerman and his group steadily worked their way toward the far shore.

Moments later an enlisted man named Alex Drabik, who had run frantically across the span in search of a missing buddy, became the first American to set foot on the east bank of the Rhine. Timmerman, following seconds later, became the first officer to cross the river.

As a bridgehead was hastily formed along the east bank, repairs were quickly made to the bridge, permitting the passage of armor to the far side. First Army commander Courtney Hodges was notified. The electrifying news was transmitted to Omar Bradley, heading the XII Army Group, then to Supreme Allied Commander Dwight Eisenhower. An elated Eisenhower authorized Bradley to put five divisions across the Rhine as quickly as possible. When Bradley pointed out that such a move was contrary to the Allies' master plan, Eisenhower roared, "To hell with the plan, Brad. Just hold that bridgehead."

The agreed-upon master plan Eisenhower referred to called for the major assault on the Rhine to be made 75 miles north of Remagen, where forces of Montgomery's XXI Army Group were poised for a late March crossing.

Since February, Montgomery had been building strength along the west bank after dual campaigns had taken his forces to the river. The operations, known as Veritable and Grenade, had seen 400,000 Canadian and British troops drive to the Rhine between Rhineberg and Rees, while American forces of William Simpson's U.S. IX Army, attached to Montgomery, had battled to the west bank at Wesel, a few miles to the south.

The Allied strategy now called for the launching of Operation Plunder, in which Montgomery would lead a powerful thrust across the Rhine and into Germany's industrial Ruhr. On his right, Simpson's IX Army would also cross, keeping pace with Montgomery's advance and protecting his right flank.

While Montgomery conducted this massive operation, Bradley's I and III armies, also at the Rhine after difficult and costly campaigns, were to assume essentially defensive positions.

Montgomery's set-piece crossing rankled not only Bradley, but his two army commanders, Hodges and Patton, as well. Plunder, they knew, was largely a British operation, one that Monty had championed since long before the fall of Paris. It meant that while the British drove into the Ruhr, the bulk of America's forces would have to remain in place, crossing the Rhine only after Montgomery was well into Germany.

Bradley had strongly advocated an alternative plan—one providing for a "double thrust" into the Reich, with Hodges and Patton crossing south of Montgomery, then driving northeast through Frankfurt and Kassel to link up with the British and Canadians in a massive encirclement of the Ruhr. But Monty, with the strong support of Winston Churchill, resisted the "double thrust" strategy, even rejecting out of hand a proposal by Gen. Simpson to cross his IX Army to the Rhine's east bank early in March. Montgomery, it seemed, was determined that the operation would be a crowning British achievement—with his northern crossing the sole "full-blooded" effort to bring Germany to her knees. Whether in the interests of Allied harmony or because he saw it as the better plan, Eisenhower had approved Montgomery's "single thrust" strategy, even at the risk of alienating his own American subordinates.

Now, Hodges's seizure of the bridge at Remagen promised to change everything. With the I Army's bridgehead across the Rhine growing stronger by the hour, Bradley was confident that his "double thrust" strategy would be considered anew.

On March 22nd, as Montgomery finalized plans for his grandiose crossing two days hence, George Patton restlessly prowled his own positions along the Rhine's west bank, 125 miles to the south.

Patton knew that the performance of his III Army since the July breakout at St. Lo had been nothing short of spectacular. In a series of lightning thrusts, it had raced across France, sealed the lower half of the Falaise pocket, then crossed the Seine and streaked to the German border. There, it had pummeled the vaunted Siegfried fortifications and reached the Rhine at Anderbach on March 9th.

Hodges's bridgehead at Remagen had indeed prompted Eisenhower to reexamine Montgomery's "single thrust" strategy. In so doing, he had quietly approved Bradley's plan for a second, southerly thrust into the Ruhr by the I and III armies.

But, for the moment, Montgomery was in the spotlight and making the most of it. Patton knew that the dignitaries had already gathered to watch the spectacle being orchestrated up north. When Montgomery and Simpson reached the other side, he realized, only he and Alex Patch, leading the U.S. VII Army on his right, would be left on the west bank. It galled him to think that the egomaniacal Montgomery would get across before he did.

For a long time Patton stared across at the eastern shore of the river. Then, with the look of a little boy who had just stumbled upon the Christmas presents, he jumped into his jeep and raced northward.

The next morning, at his headquarters in Namur, Belgium, Omar Bradley, breakfasting alone, pored over the latest summaries from the battle front.

All eyes, he knew, were on Montgomery and his much-ballyhooed Rhine crossing scheduled for the following day. Privately, Bradley agreed with Gen. George Marshall, who had complained of getting "an overdose of Montgomery" in the American press. While he hoped that Monty's crossing would go well, he was personally delighted that Courtney Hodges had grabbed the prize first.

Midway through his coffee, a telephone call from Patton brought startling news. The elated III Army commander reported that he had put his 5th Division across the Rhine on the previous night. Patton asked Bradley to withhold the news. "I don't think the Germans know I'm across yet." He laughed.

Later that day, after firmly securing his bridgehead at Oppenheim, an exultant Patton called again, urging that the news be released immediately. "Brad," he said. "I want the whole world to know that the III Army got across before Montgomery."

On the morning of March 24th, following an all-night artillery barrage and preliminary crossings by spearhead units, Montgomery sent the main elements of his XXI Army Group across the

Rhine behind a cordon of smoke that stretched for miles. At the same time, elements of the 18th Airborne Corps were dropped several miles behind the enemy front to harass the weakened German forces guarding the far side.

To the south, in a coordinated assault, Simpson's U.S. IX Army launched elements of its 16th Corps across the river.

The operation was every bit as spectacular as expected. Winston Churchill, an ever-present cigar clamped in his mouth, watched as more than 1,300 glider sorties carried the American and British paratroopers toward their drop zones. Later, when Montgomery's British II Army, supported by the Canadian 2nd Corps, had established itself on the Rhine's eastern shore and was advancing against limited opposition, Churchill released a message praising Montgomery's "first assault crossing of the Rhine in modern history." By then, however, most of the world knew that Hodges and Patton were already well entrenched on the other side.

By month's end the two armies of Jacob Devers' VI Army Group were also across the Rhine. Both Patch's VII and de Lattre's French I made successful crossings and instituted operations on the eastern side.

Less than 10 months after the landings at Normandy, the battle for the Rhine was over. The final weeks of the European war were now at hand.

The situation for Germany had grown desperate. Hitler's insistence upon a prolonged defense west of the Rhine had ravaged his already-weakened armies. No longer able to hold the natural line of the river, they could only fall back, deeper into Germany.

Field Marshal Albert Kesselring, rushed from the Italian front to replace Von Runstedt, struggled to regroup his retreating forces for a stand somewhere west of the Elbe. But this was not Italy; the crafty Kesselring had no Gustav Line or Monte Cassino at which to stop the Allied advance. Germany's entire western front, he knew, was in danger of disintegrating.

With Montgomery across the Rhine in the north, both Hodges and Patton launched Operation Voyage, an offensive aimed at breaking out of their respective bridgeheads at Remagen and Oppenheim.

Hodges's I Army spearheads thrust north and east toward Paderborn, seeking a linkup with Simpson's IX Army, which was moving south and east from Wesel. At the same time, Patton's 12th Corps advanced in the general direction of Frankfurt and Kassel.

On April 1st, when elements of the IX and I armies linked at Lippstadt, the gigantic pocket around the Ruhr was sealed. Inside the circle, more than 300,000 men of Field Marshal Walther Model's Army Group B were now cut off from their armies in the east.

As in the earlier pocket at Falaise, the Germans put up an obstinate defense. Determined attempts were made to break out of the circle, particularly at Hamm in the north and Siegen in the south. Both these efforts were turned back by American forces.

As the action intensified, the 18th Airborne Corps also entered the battle. On April 14th, the pocket was split in two. Several days later, the eastern half collapsed. Eighty thousand Germans surrendered within 24 hours. On April 18th the last organized resistance in the Ruhr pocket was snuffed out.

The catastrophic defeat had cost the Germans 325,000 prisoners. Equipment beyond measure had been destroyed or captured. Thirty general officers surrendered. One who didn't was Walther Model. Telling an aide, "A field marshal must never become a prisoner," he walked into a forest north of Dusseldorf and shot himself.

By the time resistance in the Ruhr pocket had been extinguished, the rest of Hitler's armies were already 100 miles to the east. The German retreat had become a rout.

For his plan following the Rhine crossing, Eisenhower had decided that the main Allied push would be toward Leipzig, aimed at cutting Germany in two and preventing the passage of enemy forces into the south.

This decision was prompted, among other things, by Eisenhower's deep concern over reports that Hitler and some of his key aides planned to move a number of elite panzer and SS divisions into a National Redoubt in the mountainous regions of western Austria for a suicidal final stand. The Führer's Bavarian mountain retreat at Berchtesgaden, it was reported, would serve as the command post.

This National Redoubt theory had strong supporters among many of Eisenhower's top aides, Bradley among them. While such a situation failed to develop—owing largely to the speed with which Allied forces cut across Germany—fears of an Austrian "last stand" by Hitler and his cronies persisted until war's end.

In his role as Allied Supreme Commander, Eisenhower had made another key decision, one that would affect the political shape of the postwar world.

With the Russians moving rapidly westward in a sweeping final offensive, Eisenhower was anxious to link up with them and prevent German combat units retreating to the east and west from joining forces. In order to hasten such a meeting, he had decided not to advance on Berlin, the German capital and seat of Nazi power.

Berlin, he felt, was a shell, without military value. Russian forces were already closing in on the city. It was doubtful that American units could reach it in time. Beyond that, Eisenhower had estimated that such a campaign would be needlessly costly—that the Allied war effort would be better served by a steady advance to the Elbe, there to join with Stalin's armies and close out the war.

His plan found many dissenters—Churchill among them—men who feared the consequences of a Russian seizure of the German capital and its effect on the postwar world. But Eisenhower was not to be deterred. Although he ordered Simpson's IX Army to be ready to strike for Berlin at a moment's notice, he stood by his difficult decision until war's end.

From the North Sea to Austria, the Allied front moved inexorably forward.

While Canadian First Army forces swung into Holland and northern Germany, troops of the British II Army moved toward the North Sea ports of Kiel and Lubeck.

Having lost the services of the U.S. IX Army—which had been returned to Bradley's XII Army Group—Montgomery plodded eastward at a snail's pace, his heart no longer in the fight. Relegated to a supporting role after his magnificently staged crossing of the Rhine, the British field marshal now advanced with his usual caution, giving rise to grave concerns within SHAEF headquarters.

There were widespread fears that German units in the north might flee into Denmark or Norway. Only a rapid advance to the Baltic by Montgomery could close off these escape routes. It was only after constant prodding by Eisenhower and the addition of Ridgeway's 18th Airborne Corps to his command that Monty was able to accomplish his mission.

To Montgomery's right, Bill Simpson's IX Army, having sealed the northern half of the Ruhr pocket, drove on, south of Munster, to reach the Elbe near Magdeberg. Simpson was now only 65 miles from Berlin.

In the center, Hodges's advance also moved with breathtaking speed, slowed only by determined resistance that developed in the area of the Harz Mountains. On April 19th, Leipzig fell. Hodges's 69th division now had a clear path to the Mulde River.

In the south, while Patton's III Army dashed for the Austrian frontier, Patch's VII overran Bavaria.

At the southern extreme of the Allied line, de Lattre's French I Army blazed through the Black Forest, their sights set on Stuttgart.

As the Allied drive pressed forward, one great city after another fell. Bremen, Hamburg, Nuremberg, and Munich were overwhelmed by Eisenhower's onrushing armies.

German units were now surrendering en masse. During the first three weeks of April, more than a million prisoners were taken. Allied POW compounds were filled to overflowing.

On April 25th a patrol of the 273rd Regiment of the 69th Division, probing eastward from the Mulde, met up with elements of the Russian 58th Guards Division in the area of Torgau on the Elbe. The western and eastern fronts had at last been joined.

With their communications a shambles, German resistance now deteriorated into small actions by independent commands. Sector after sector collapsed. For the average German soldier, further resistance seemed futile.

On April 30th, with his world collapsing around him, Adolf Hitler prowled his bunker deep beneath the ruins of Berlin, hoping for a miracle. None was forthcoming.

Finally, with Russian armored units only yards away, the Führer said goodbye to his staff, then retired to his private quarters with Eva Braun, his wife of 24 hours. Moments later, after she had taken poison, Hitler fired a Waltham pistol into his mouth. The towering symbol of the Third Reich was no more.

The two bodies were carried to a garden outside the bunker. With Russian artillery shells falling nearby, the corpses were doused with gasoline and set afire.

Beyond the high walls, Berlin lay in ruins. All across the gutted city, thick smoke swirled slowly toward the shrouded sky mixing with all the grim finality of that rising from the pitiful, smoldering heap in the garden of the Führerbunker.

At 0241 on May 7, 1945, in the war room of SHAEF's headquarters at Rheims, General Alfred Jodl signed the instruments of unconditional surrender.

On May 9th, at one minute after midnight, all hostilities

ceased. The war in Europe was over.

American casualties totaled 586,628 men, of whom 135,576 gave their lives.

Osthoffen, France, January 30, 1945. A 12th Armored Division's jeep plows the snow and drifts to reach its objective.

Krinkolt, Belgium, January 31, 1945. Company K of the 38th Infantry, 2nd Infantry Division, hits the snow to avoid incoming artillery fire.

Oberhoffen, France, February 3, 1945. Soldier passes a tank destroyer used in support of infantry to blast Germans out of buildings. The unit is from the 14th Armored Division.

February 3, 1945. 2nd Infantry Division patrol in the ruins of Harperscheid.

Magueneu, France, February 5, 1945. Company L, 313rd Infantry, 79th Division. Mortar shells explode on enemy positions across the Moder River.

February 9, 1945. 301st Regiment, 49th Infantry Division troops, under heavy fire, run for shelter in a wrecked building.

Siegfried Line, Habschied, Germany, February 12, 1945. The 358th Regiment of the 90th Infantry Division pass the concrete dragon's teeth of the Siegfried Line as they move up to the front.

February 14, 1945. Men of a field artillery unit near Saarlautern, Germany, repair a break in a field wire. At left is Pvt. Norman G. Wirth, of Strasberg, Ill.; and on the right, Cpl. Emry Dzerbicki, of Detroit.

Kleinhan, Germany. Pvt. Frederick F. Oxen-reivi, of Tendle, Pa., carries a load of hay to line his foxhole. February 1945.

Roer River. This bridge was blown up by the Germans during the first wave of assault troops of the 104th Infantry Division. Assault boats are scattered about. February 23, 1945.

Roer River, February 24, 1945. 1st Army tank dozers of the 104th Division make a crossing over the Roer treadway bridge.

February 1945. The Bitburg Raid. The heavy bombing of Bitburg, Germany, helped the 5th Division of the I Army to take the town.

Pirmasens, Germany, 1945. The 8th Air Force's continuous bombing left few walls standing. The enemy was softened up and the city fell relatively easily to the 66th Regiment of the 71st Infantry Division.

Para-Infantrymen of the Eighty-second Airborne Division with British Second Army cross the Elbe River in a Buffalo. This was the last water barrier between airborne soldiers and Berlin.

March 2, 1945. I. G. Farbenindustrie Plant at Oppau, Germany. The results of bombing by the 8th U.S. Air Force.

March 2, 1945. A tank dozer of the 8th Armored Division, U.S. IX Army, mows down German tank traps.

Forbach, France, March 3, 1945. A 276th Infantry, 70th Division combat medic races across a village road raked by enemy fire. His buddies are giving him fire support.

March 3, 1945. 2nd Army units move through Krefeld, Germany.

March 4, 1945. Troops of the 424th Infantry Regiment, survivors of The Battle of the Bulge, as guidons are presented to reconstituted units of the division.

Roer River, Uerdingan, Germany. GI's of the 379th Infantry Regiment, 95th Infantry Division, fire across the river from a waterfront cafe. March 5, 1945.

Fletrange region, France, March 9, 1945. 134th Ordnance Battalion, 14th Armored Division's rocket launchers mounted on a Sherman M-4A3 fire test rockets.

Germany, March 9, 1945. 2nd Battalion, 2nd Infantry Division troops under heavy fire from the enemy as they move against them.

March 9, 1945. While machine gunners set up their .30 caliber machine guns, GI's of the 28th Division dash across a stream at Weldau, Germany. The 26th Division forded the Schleuse River to assault enemy troops in the surrounding forests.

Herne, Germany, March 9, 1945. Infantrymen of the 35th Division advance cautiously along streets where they are under heavy fire.

Hanover, Germany, March 10, 1945. U.S. Ninth Army tanks and infantry pass dead Nazis. The GI's belong to the 84th Division.

March 14, 1945. 5th Division infantrymen cross the Moselle on assault rafts.

Roer River, Shaphoven, Germany. The 2nd Battalion, 20th Regiment, 30th Infantry Division cross the river on a footbridge.

March 14, 1945. Firing at enemy positions at Windischleuba, Germany.

Vazig, Germany, March 15, 1945. Cpl. Edward Meares, from Chicago, stands watch with his 57mm antitank gun. Below him is the Moselle River.

March 15, 1945. 4th Armored Division vehicles cross the Moselle River on a "treadway" bridge.

Siegfried Line, March 20, 1945. 63rd Division troops climb over tank obstacles near Wurzbach. The unit is from A Company, 255th Infantry Regiment.

March 20, 1945. German prisoners in an enclosure in Germany.

Rhine River at Ludwigshafen, March 25, 1945. German shells land on this once-important industrial city. Before it was taken by the Allies, it was a constant bombing target.

Oberwesel on Rhine River, March 26, 1945. 89th Division soldiers crouch low in their DUKW craft to avoid enemy fire during the crossing.

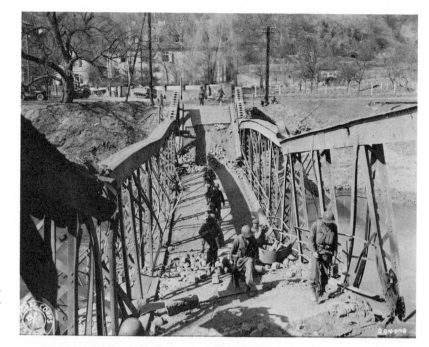

March 28, 1945. Infantry of U.S. I Army, 2nd Battalion, 38th Regiment, 2nd Infantry Division cross a wrecked bridge at Nor-Bieber, Germany.

Company E, Second Battalion troops ferret out sniper left to slow up advancing Allied units, March 28, 1945. Ludwigshafen.

Rhine River, near Mainz, Germany, March 29, 1945. 80th Division men and equipment load into landing craft prior to crossing the Rhine.

April 1, 1945. A rocket tank was very successful at the Fula River.

April 3, 1945. P-47's support the 42nd Division by dropping 500-lb. bombs on enemy strong points.

April 9, 1945. Troops of the 325th Infantry Regiment of the 9th Infantry Division move carefully into just-captured Saalhausen, en route to the Ruhr pocket.

Geraberg, Germany, April 12, 1945. 565th Division infantrymen move through a wooded area following retreating German soldiers.

April 19, 1945. The 3rd Division tanks under heavy fire in Nuremberg.

Third Division Tank-Infantry team mopping up enemy troops in Nuremberg, April 19, 1945.

Tanks roll through the razed city of Nuremberg, April 19, 1945.

April 19, 1945. Precision bombing saved the Magdeberg Cathedral.

April 1945. This damaged B-17 landed safely after losing its nose to German antiaircraft flak guns.

April 20, 1945, Nuremberg, Germany. 180th Infantry Regiment soldiers of the 45th Division clean out snipers with the help of tanks.

Wernberg, Germany, April 22, 1945. One of the 22nd Tank Battalion stands ready in front of a house that his guns set afire.

Masau, Austria, April 29, 1945. 3rd Battalion, 71st Regiment, 44th Division troops move from the foothills into the Tyrolean Alps. Their objective: to clear out pockets of German resistance.

April 30, 1945. Germans surrendering to 3rd Division GI's near Munich.

Weiden, Germany, May 1, 1945. The body of a slave laborer killed during a death march from Flossenburg concentration camp. Unable to march, hundreds were shot or beaten to death by their SS Guards. The investigating soldiers are from the 97th Division.

May 1, 1945. 103rd Infantry Division troops advance into Schnaritz, Austria, after a heavy artillery preparation.

May 3, 1945. This tank of the 7th Armored Division wets its tracks in the Baltic Sea at Rehna, Germany. The tankmen were the first Americans to reach the Baltic Sea.

Berchtesgaden, May 4, 1945. 3rd Armored Division tanks and infantry enter the town.

Braunau, Austria. 317th Infantry Regiment of the 80th Infantry Division cross the Imm River on pontoon bridge put in place by the 305th Engineers.

May 1945. 9th Division Infantry firing at the enemy near Morsbach.

May 1945. Troops crossing the Weser River to attack Furstenberg.

May 1945. Covering advance troops in house-to-house fighting in Bruhl, Germany.

May 1945. A royal observation post. These GI's have set up shop in Kaiser Wilhelm's Palace in Bruhl.

May 5, 1945. Checking for snipers in a small Austrian village.

May 1945. Preparing to cross the Elbe River near Torgau.

Rheims, France, May 6, 1945. SHAEF War Room. Lt. Gen. Carl A. Spaatz, Commanding General U.S. Tactical Air Force, and Maj. Gen. Ivan Susloparoff, Russian Chief of Staff, sign Nazi unconditional surrender document.

Rheims, May 6, 1945. Lt. Gen. Walter Bedell Smith, Allied Chief of Staff, signs the document posing unconditional surrender of the Wehrmacht. At Supreme Allied Headquarters at Rheims.

Rheims, May 6, 1945. Adm. George von Fridenberg, Commander in Chief of the German Fleet and spokesman for Gross Admiral Doenitz, arrives at SHAEF Headquarters to receive and discuss unconditional surrender terms.

Rheims, May 7, 1945. Unconditional surrender signed by Gen. Alfred Jodl, Wehrmacht Chief of Staff. Maj. Wilhelm Erenius, his aide, at left; Adm. George von Fridenberg, Commander in Chief of the German Navy.

Rheims, May 7, 1945. Gen. Alfred Jodl, German Chief of Staff under Admiral Doenitz, signs document of unconditional surrender.

SHAEF Headquarters. Gen. Alfred Jodl, German Chief of Staff (center, back to camera) signs unconditional surrender. To his left, Adm. von Fridenberg; to his right, his aide. Across the table, left to right: Lt. Gen. Sir F. E. Morgan, Deputy Chief of Staff; General Francois Saves (Representing Gen. Alphonse Juin); Adm. Harold E. Burroughs, Commander in Chief Allied Naval Expeditionary Force; Lt. Gen. Artillery Ivan Susloparoff, Soviet Representative; Gen. Carl A. Spaatz, CG USSTAF; Air Marshal H. R. Bull, Asst. Chief of Staff G-3, SHAEF; and Senior Gen. Lt. Col. Ivan Zenkovitch, interpreter.

Marshal Georgi K. Zhukov, Commander in Chief of all Soviet Forces, signs the ratified unconditional surrender terms as agreed upon in Rheims. May 9, 1945.

Belz, France. The Lorient Pocket was held by 28,000 Germans from June 1944 until May 7, 1945. Here Col. John Gavin, Chief of Staff, 66th Division, along with French officers accepts the surrender of the Lorient Pocket.

Col. Borst, the Commander of the German troops, signs documents. Seated opposite are Col. Gavin and Col. John Keating. The German officer nearest the camera is Lt. Sparig.

May 9, 1945. Lt. Gen. Fahrmnbacker, commander of the port since 1944, surrenders to Maj. Gen. Herman Krummer, 66th Division Commander.

May 9, 1945. Reich Marshal Hermann Göring surrenders to 7th Army forces. Here he arrives at camp in Augsberg, Germany.

Linz, Austria. General George S. Patton, Commanding General, U.S. Third Army, and General Nikonor Zahwatgaeff, Commanding General, Russian Guard Army, salute as they pass the Stars and Stripes.

THE WAR IN THE PACIFIC

CHAPTER **8** THE BATTLE OF MIDWAY: STEMMING THE TIDE

"Do you see what I see?"

—PBY pilot to co-pilot after sighting Midway attack force.

From the bridge of his flagship, the *Yamato*, Admiral Isoroku Yamamoto watched as the island of Hashirajima, nestled between the main islands of Honshu and Shikoku, disappeared into the wispy morning fog.

Uncharacteristically tense, the Commander in Chief of the Imperial Japanese Fleet considered his hazardous mission and prayed silently that he might return to his home base in glorious victory. Still, the icy hand of uncertainty lay heavily upon him.

He turned to face the bow, his gaze sweeping lovingly across the awesome expanse of the *Yamato*. With her deadly weaponry, including nine 18-inch guns, the battleship was the world's most powerful war machine. Yamamoto watched in admiration as her 64,000 tons cut cleanly through the calm Pacific at more than 27 knots.

The day, May 28, 1942, had dawned crisp and clear except for some very high cirrus clouds that now drifted lazily away from the coast toward the eastern horizon. Six hundred miles beyond its hazy line, Vice Admiral Chuichi Nagumo, leading the First Carrier Strike Force, was already racing toward the mission's principal target, the American naval base at Midway Island. A diversionary force was en route to the Aleutians.

Yamamoto knew that Midway's capture would open the way for Japanese attacks against Hawaii and the western United States. And none too soon. American industry was booming. Time was running out.

As the bridge crackled with departure orders, the admiral stepped outside to catch the last of the cool morning breeze. Ahead, the battleships *Nagato* and *Mutsu* commanded the horizon. Escort ships dotted the sparkling Pacific as far as the eye could see.

Well aware that his adversary, Adm. Nimitz, was far too clever to risk the American fleet with a deep incursion into the western Pacific, Yamamoto had decided to seek him out—to draw him into battle. Nimitz, he knew, would not sit idly by and watch Midway, America's Pacific sentry, fall. Despite his lesser strength, he would have to fight. Yamamoto would soon have his long-sought confrontation with the remnants of the U.S. fleet. He would finish the job started at Pearl Harbor.

Despite his tenseness, he knew there was much to be thankful for. Everywhere, the war was going well. In the six months since the attack on Hawaii, the Japanese war machine had rolled across the western Pacific adding victory to stunning victory. But the army, normally the more militant branch, now seemed content merely to lie back and consolidate gains previously won.

Yamamoto would have none of that. It was imperative that Japan strike a decisive blow before America's weapons of war, already pouring out of U.S. factories, began to make themselves felt. Yamamoto was a realist. If America was not defeated by the end of 1942, the war was lost.

Shielding his eyes, he watched as a flight of low-flying bombers—bound for an airbase on Shikoku—approached. Wing tips glinted in the bright sunlight. The drone of the powerful engines brought to mind another flight that had swept over Japan six weeks before. Curiously, Col. Jimmy Doolittle's raid on Tokyo had played right into his hands. With the army having steadfastly refused to allocate the troops necessary to invade Australia—part of his master plan—Yamamoto had all but given up hope for continued Japanese expansion. But Col. Doolittle's arrogant violation of the Japanese homeland had dramatically demonstrated a pressing need for the extension of Japan's defensive perimeter and the destruction of the American fleet that now threatened the home islands. Strange, Yamamoto thought. With all his military power, all his influence with the emperor himself, he had been unable to achieve what had been wrought with one bold stroke by an American colonel and a handful of his airmen.

The wind seemed to rise. Signal flags atop the *Yamato*'s tall masts snapped in the stiff breeze. Dark thunder clouds appeared on the eastern horizon. Sadly, Yamamoto recalled the earlier, first phase of his present mission, one intended to establish a base on southern New Guinea. Not only had it ended in failure, but two of his fleet carriers, badly damaged in the action, had been unable to join him in the Midway strike. But the encounter had cost the Americans the carrier *Lexington*, a loss they could ill afford.

Yamamoto knew there was little with which Nimitz could stop him. The impending battle would be won through superior strength, secrecy, and surprise. Japanese naval might would, *must* prevail.

The thought gave him respite from the morning's tensions and a new confidence emerged. In spite of the deteriorating weather, he felt pleasantly renewed. With a last, lingering look at his majestic fleet, Isoroku Yamamoto returned to the bridge.

Had Adm. Yamamoto been aware of the frantic activity taking place in an inconspicuous low brick building at Pearl Harbor's Naval Base, his new feelings of confidence would have quickly eroded.

There, in a series of brightly lit rooms, high-ranking American naval officers were carefully analyzing intercepted Japanese communications indicating that the strike at Midway was underway.

Months earlier, American cryptographers had broken the Japanese naval code. Several weeks before the crucial engagement in the Coral Sea, Adm. Chester Nimitz had been advised of Yamamoto's broad plan—a strike at Port Moresby, New Guinea, landings at Tulagi, in the Solomons, then a mammoth naval assault against Midway. With the Coral Sea behind them and Yamamoto's strength now committed to the Midway attack, Nimitz's staff had quickly organized a naval force with which to meet the threat. Despite the limited resources, 76 warships had been assembled from various commands. The American fleet was now ready to meet the challenge.

Nimitz was convinced that he could beat the Japanese at their own game. With Yamamoto unaware that his naval code had been broken, he would sail boldy toward Midway, certain that no American carriers would be in the area. Further, Nimitz was encouraged by news that the carrier *Yorktown*, severely damaged in the Coral Sea action, had been miraculously repaired at Pearl Harbor in little more than 48 hours. She would be ready for sea momentarily. Another surprise awaiting Yamamoto, Nimitz thought. He had a lot of them coming.

Before sundown on May 28th, as Yamamoto and Nagumo closed for the attack, Nimitz ordered Task Force 16, under Rear Adm. Raymond A. Spruance, to sail immediately for Midway.

Spruance, who had taken over for the ailing "Bull" Halsey, was admittedly nervous, never having commanded a ship in combat. But his force was formidable and included the fleet carriers *Hornet* and *Enterprise*.

Rear Adm. Frank Jack Fletcher, the veteran commander of Task Force 17, was ordered to follow Spruance aboard the *Yorktown* within 48 hours.

In the cryptanalysis section, lights burned late into the night. Japanese naval messages were scrutinized over and over. Tension was high. Within the stifling confines of the small building, a chilling realization was shared by all: The Pacific Fleet was sailing toward a confrontation that could well decide the future course of the war.

High above the *Yorktown*'s flight deck, Adm. Fletcher, eyes glued to the horizon, leaned back in his chair.

Somewhere beyond the light mist hugging the Pacific, Ray Spruance and Task Force 16 were waiting. After a moment, Fletcher leaned forward and placed his eyes against the high-powered binoculars fixed to a stand next to his chair. Slowly, he scanned the ocean, eager for some sign of the *Hornet* and *Enterprise*, backbone of Spruance's force. Nothing.

It was June 2nd. Task Force 17's position was approximately 350 miles northeast of Midway. With Nagumo closing fast, Fletcher's orders were clear: Rendezvous with Spruance, then move north of Midway—out of range of Japanese search planes—to await the first sighting of Nagumo's fleet by Midway patrol craft.

Below him, service crews swarmed about a squadron of F4U Corsairs, propellers turning, poised for takeoff in the event of an enemy sighting. Behind them, ordnance crews trundled bombs across the vast flight deck before loading them beneath the bellies of the SBD's, the Navy's deadly dive bombers. Fletcher sensed that the entire ship was boiling with excitement and anticipation. That was good. The added adrenalin would serve his men well in the crucial battle that lay ahead.

As the carrier plowed through heavy seas, Fletcher's ears were attuned to every groan and creak of the stately *Yorktown*. While he had been amazed at the miraculous 48-hour repair she had undergone at Pearl, he harbored deep concern that such a schedule might have left her less than 100 percent seaworthy. Watertight seams, hastily welded, had been known to part under the shattering concussions of battle. But for the moment at least, the veteran ship, still licking her Coral Sea wounds, was responding well.

Fletcher thought of that confused, misdirected battle, fought during the first week in May. There had been costly errors on both sides. Botched communications, erroneous sighting reports, and the ever-present fickle hand of fate had contributed to a largely inconclusive result. Except that Japan's Port Moresby invasion force had been recalled, ending, for the moment, the grave threat to Australia.

Fletcher mourned the gracious *Lexington*. Her loss had been a less than equal trade for the light carrier *Shoho*, sunk by American carrier planes.

But that was then and this was now. The *Yorktown* was back— ready to avenge the "Lady Lex" and all those who had died with her.

As Adm. Fletcher removed his cap and tried to wipe the weariness from his eyes, a voice from the squawk box announced that Task Force 16 had just been sighted several miles off the port quarter. Through the bridge binoculars, he could barely make out the dim outline of an American carrier—the *Enterprise*, he thought. He checked his watch, pleased that the rendezvous with Ray Spruance was smack on schedule. Being the senior of the two, he would now take command of both forces and move the task groups, as ordered, north of Midway. Then it would be a waiting game.

Signaling his co-pilot to take the controls, Ensign Jack Reid reached for his search glasses for what seemed the hundredth time that morning. Nearly 700 miles out of Midway, his PBY *Catalina* was at the limit of its search. A quick fuel check told him he would have to turn back within minutes.

As had been the case all during the arduous flight, Reid saw nothing through his glasses but the endless Pacific. Nevertheless, he continued to scour the ocean ahead, his body aching from the long hours in the left seat.

Reid was well aware that a Japanese fleet was en route to Midway—that a major sea battle was imminent. But the scope of what was impending eluded him. During his long, claustrophobic confinement, Jack Reid's world had shrunk to include only Ensign Hardeman, his co-pilot, the maze of instruments that enveloped the two of them, and what he could see through the long-range binoculars—which up until now had been zilch— nothing.

Reid made one last sweep across the horizon, then signaled Hardeman to turn back. The co-pilot began a lazy bank toward the east. Suddenly, Reid squinted ahead, then raised the glasses once more. Something had captured his attention. Abruptly, he motioned the co-pilot to hand him control and banked the *Catalina* back on course. Flipping on the auto pilot, he handed the glasses to Hardeman. "Do you see what I see?" he said, pointing to a position on the horizon. Hardeman focused the binoculars. Thirty miles ahead, he could make out a large group of dark objects—warships and transports—all heading toward them. The young co-pilot lowered the glasses. "You're damned right I do," he replied.

The first contact with Yamamoto's fleet had been made. The Japanese Occupation Force bound for Midway had been sighted. It was 0925, June 3rd.

Dawn, June 4th. Positioned 280 miles northwest of Midway, Adm. Chuichi Nagumo ordered his four carriers to turn into the wind and launch aircraft.

From the flight decks of the *Akagi*, *Kaga*, *Hiryu*, and *Soryu*, 108 heavily armed warplanes gracefully rose into the dawn sky.

Aboard the *Akagi*, Nagumo reread a report that Adm. Kondo's Occupation Force had been sighted and attacked by American land-based bombers. He wondered if Yamamoto had picked up the communication—and if the American fleet was also aware of their presence in the area.

As a precaution, he sent search planes aloft to seek out any American warships that might be in the area. Then, calm and confident, he headed for the Combat Control Center to monitor reports of the attack on Midway.

The first crackling sounds of flight leader Joichi Tomonago's strike report were encouraging. They told Nagumo that American fighter defense over Midway had been weak. Japanese Zeros had destroyed 17 of the 26 planes that had risen to confront them. Midway's naval base had been heavily damaged. But Tomonago, now en route back to the carrier, strongly urged another attack.

Nagumo knew that his second-wave planes, still aboard the carriers, were loaded with torpedoes and armor-piercing ordnance in preparation for action against U.S. ships. Before being dispatched to Midway, they would have to be rearmed with high-explosive and fragmentation bombs. That would take precious time. As Nagumo pondered the problem, a flight of Midway-based B-17's suddenly appeared overhead. Bombing inaccurately from above 20,000 feet, their attack did little damage. But it convinced Nagumo that Tomonago had been right. He ordered the second-wave planes rearmed for another strike at Midway.

0930, June 4th. Cmdr. John Waldron, leading a flight of TBD Devastator torpedo bombers, peered through a break in the clouds and sighted Nagumo's sprawling task force. Several hours earlier, Waldron's squadron had been launched from the deck of the *Hornet* after Nagumo's position had been reported.

The commander looked about for the protective fighters that had accompanied his group. They were nowhere to be seen. Without hesitation, he ordered his unit, Torpedo #8, to attack. The lumbering, difficult-to-maneuver torpedo planes began a labored descent toward the Pacific.

Leveling off at near wave-top height, the TBD's began their torpedo runs. But Nagumo's speedy Zero fighters were quickly upon them. Within minutes, all 15 of Waldron's slow-flying planes were shot into the sea. Only one member of Torpedo #8, Ensign Tex Gay, survived the slaughter. Floating in the Pacific after he had been shot down, Gay was eyewitness to the incredible events of June 4th as the Battle of Midway unfolded all around him.

Moments after Torpedo #8 had been destroyed, 26 more TBD's, these from the *Enterprise* and *Yorktown*, appeared over Nagumo's task force. Again the Japanese Zeros did their deadly work, downing 20 of the bombers. By 1015, only 45 minutes after Waldron's squadron had arrived over the fleet, 35 of 41 Devastators had been blasted from the sky. Not one of their torpedoes had reached its target.

In the first few hours of the battle, the Japanese had destroyed 83 American planes while losing only 6 of their own. Within moments, 102 of Nagumo's second-wave torpedo and dive bombers were set to be unleashed against Midway. The admiral was joyous. A great Japanese victory was at hand. Then, with breathtaking suddenness, his luck ran out.

The SBD Dauntless dive bombers and F4F Wildcat fighters that had lost the ill-fated Torpedo #8, due to erroneous position information, arrived over Nagumo's fleet. The Zeros were still at low level, mangling the last of Waldron's doomed Devastators. At the same time, the Japanese carriers were maneuvering to avoid the slow-running American torpedoes. It was to be the decisive moment of World War II.

Attacking from above 20,000 feet, the Dauntless dive bombers plummeted toward Nagumo's ships. The Zeros had no time to rise up and meet them. In fact, the American planes were barely noticed. Only the terrifying scream of their engines gave a last-second warning before their bombs came hurtling toward the Japanese carriers. Several direct hits were scored on the flagship *Akagi*. With her decks and hangars still strewn with refueling planes and live bombs waiting to be loaded for the second strike at Midway, the ship was racked by thunderous explosions. Within moments, Nagumo ordered her abandoned. He and his staff were taken off the carrier.

A few miles away, the *Kaga* met a similar fate as four bombs from another flight of SBD's found their mark. She was soon a raging inferno.

At the same moment, dive bombers from the *Yorktown* located the *Soryu*. By 1040 her rudder and engines had been blasted out of action and uncontrollable fires raged throughout the ship.

The stunned, enraged Nagumo signaled his only operational carrier, the *Hiryu*, to launch planes for a retaliatory strike at the American fleet, which had now been sighted by his searchers. Forty planes in two waves took off to attack Fletcher and Spruance. As they gained altitude, the Japanese pilots soberly watched the burning hulks of their three devastated carriers.

Shortly before noon, standing on the bridge of the *Yorktown*, Capt. Elliott Buckmaster, commanding, watched as the tiny black dots on the horizon grew larger. Having already launched his fighters, he could do nothing but wait.

The *Yorktown*'s antiaircraft batteries opened up. Combat communications told Buckmaster that 6, then 9, then 12 Japanese fighters and dive bombers had been downed.

But the *Yorktown* was not to escape again. She shuddered as three bombs from Japanese Val dive bombers found their mark. Fires erupted everywhere. The big carrier went dead in the water. Concerned that his hastily repaired ship might take on water and capsize, Buckmaster advised Adm. Fletcher to transfer his flag to the cruiser *Astoria*, standing by.

Later, aboard the *Astoria*, Fletcher watched the billowing smoke from the *Yorktown*. Coldly, he ordered search planes from the *Enterprise* to find the *Hiryu*.

At 1445, the same moment that Fletcher's search planes sighted the *Hiryu*, a flight of Japanese torpedo planes, flying low through heavy fire, put two torpedoes into the *Yorktown*, which had just gotten underway. All power connections were severed. The huge carrier developed a dangerous list. Still concerned about the ship's watertight integrity, Buckmaster ordered her abandoned. But the old carrier proved difficult to kill. Taken under tow by an American minesweeper, the stricken *Yorktown* was again limping back to Pearl when torpedoed and sunk by a Japanese submarine two days later.

The final, dramatic moments of the Battle of Midway were at hand. At 1700 on June 4th, 24 American dive bombers, some refugees from the mortally wounded *Yorktown*, struck the *Hiryu*. Although her Zeros defended vigorously, four American bombs found their mark. Planes on the flight deck began burning furiously. The last of Nagumo's carriers was doomed.

Between 1900 and 1930 hours on June 4th, both the *Soryu* and the *Kaga* disappeared beneath the waters of the Pacific. The following day, on orders from Yamamoto, the *Akagi* and *Hiryu* were sent to the bottom by Japanese torpedoes. Rear Admiral Tamon Yamaguchi, the *Hiryu's* commander, the officer who was said to be the logical successor to Yamamoto, obstinately refused to leave his post and perished, tied to the carrier's bridge.

At 0200 on June 5th, aboard the battleship *Yamato*, a weary, somber Yamamoto studied the combat reports from the battle area. It was now clear that no hope remained. The impossible had happened. Even the successful diversionary landings on Kiska and Attu were little consolation. Although that northern task force was racing southward to assist him, Yamamoto knew that his plan to capture Midway and destroy the U.S. fleet had failed. There was nothing to stop the Americans now. Soon her industrial might would flood the battle zone with weapons of war. In contrast, Japan was incapable of replacing the wreckage, human and otherwise, that now lay beneath the Pacific. There was no longer any doubt. Japan had lost the war. It would be a long, sad journey back to Hashirajima.

At 0255, on June 5th, 1942, having ordered a general withdrawal from the battle zone, Isoroku Yamamoto, stoic in defeat, retired to his cabin to ponder the inevitable fate of his beloved homeland and the torturous days that lay ahead.

A TBN flying over the bow of USS *Yorktown*.
May 1942.

May 1942. The CV-5 USS *Yorktown* heads
toward the Japanese fleet.

Ensigns Reid and Hardeman banked their Catalina aircraft at the end of the sweep. "Do you see what I see?" Reid asked, indicating a large group of dark objects. They were approaching warships and transports. The Battle of Midway was beginning. It was June 2, 1942.

CV-6 USS *Enterprise*, at high speed in the Battle of Midway. June 4, 1942

USS *Yorktown*, hit by a torpedo on the port side during the Japanese attacks of June 4, 1942.

USS *Yorktown*, under attack and burning.

USS *Yorktown*, showing damage during the early phase of the Battle of Midway.

USS *Yorktown*, bombed on June 4, 1942.

The USS *Yorktown*. Crew members and fliers examine the damage done by the Japanese air raiders in the Battle of Midway. The *Yorktown* suffered her deathblow when struck by torpedoes from an enemy submarine.

USS *Yorktown*, sinking.

Abandoned, USS *Yorktown* takes water. Shortly after this photograph was taken, "The Fighting Lady" sank beneath the Pacific waves.

CHAPTER 9 GUADALCANAL: THE FIRST OFFENSIVE

"A malaria-ridden place of death."

—Jack London's description of Guadalcanal Island.

From his command post beneath a sheltering stand of coconut palms, Maj. Gen. Alexander A. Vandergrift watched in dismay as troops of his 1st Marine Division stumbled through an amphibious assault against the immaculate, sunswept coast of Fiji Island. His binoculars swept the sea off the white-sand beach as hundreds of Higgins boats and tracked landing vehicles (amtracs) dizzily crisscrossed each other in a tortuous approach to shore, then mercifully disgorged their pitiful cargos—a sprawling, retching mass of seasick marines.

The invasion rehearsal had been a shambles. With assault landings at Guadalcanal—scheduled for August 7, 1942—only weeks away, Vandergrift regretted having agreed to the impossibly short schedule. Watching yet another wave of boats cross the line of departure and proceed uncertainly toward shore, he sought consolation in the old show business adage, "Bad dress rehearsal, good show."

Ever since America's brilliant naval victories in the Coral Sea and at Midway, the pace of the Japanese war had quickened dramatically. With the enemy's advance finally stopped, all efforts were now focused on the nation's first Pacific offensive, at Guadalcanal. It was a critical moment in the conduct of the war and Vandergrift was proud that his marines had been chosen to lead the way. But their shabby performance on this crystal clear Fiji afternoon certainly gave cause for alarm if not panic.

Forty minutes later, having suffered through the final landing rehearsals, a gruff, ill-tempered Vandergrift called for a meeting of all divisional commanders for early evening. Those who watched his somber departure knew that congratulations would not be part of the general's agenda.

Late that afternoon Vandergrift, lean and erect, strode from his temporary quarters to face a blazing Melanesian sunset. He paused to drink in its beauty, weary from the terrible burdens of the past weeks.

Summoned to Auckland five weeks earlier, he had been ordered to get his division combat ready by the first week in August. When told the target—Guadalcanal—he didn't even know where it was. The only maps of the 90- by 25-mile mountainous jungle island at the southern end of the Solomon chain predated World War I. Estimates of enemy defenses were at best educated guesses. But American reconnaissance planes had reported an airfield being rushed to completion posing a grave threat to America's Australian lifeline. If a planned two-pronged Allied offensive aimed at the Japanese home islands was to succeed, it was imperative that Australia, one of the jumping-off points, be protected. The other base for the Pacific advance was Guadalcanal. Only when Japan's brief occupation of that island was ended could the offensive begin.

Plans had been rushed to completion with such speed and with so few forces available that the invasion had been nicknamed Operation Shoestring. Recognizing the importance of his assignment, Vandergrift was confident that his marines would go ashore and take the measure of the fanatical Japanese, acknowledged to be the best jungle fighters in the world—until now.

His spirits revived by the glorious Fiji sunset, Vandergrift strode briskly toward the pea-green Quonset hut at the far end of the placid beach. He had made his decision. The meeting would be brief—no hell raising, just a few solid suggestions on how to improve their performance, then urge them to get on with it. And they would. His marines would get the job done.

Watching as the big naval guns thundered their missiles toward Guadalcanal, Rear Adm. Richmond K. Turner's feelings of unease continued to mount. As commander of the Solomons invasion force, he was acutely aware of his place in history. Within moments, 18,000 marines aboard his 23 transports would begin the first American land offensive of the Pacific war. But even as the assault troops loaded into their boats, Turner's concern over Japanese naval control of the area continued to plague him. Certainly, Japan's crafty naval chief, Adm. Yamamoto, would boldly contest this first intrusion on Japanese-held territory. And Rabaul, the powerful enemy naval base on New Britain Island, was less than a day's sailing.

True, Adm. Frank Jack Fletcher's Task Force #61 was standing by south of Guadalcanal; even now, planes from its carriers—the *Wasp*, *Saratoga*, and *Enterprise*—were sweeping the shoreline in sustained prelanding attacks. But Turner feared that Fletcher would be no match for a well-timed naval strike from Rabaul. With much of America's Pacific Fleet having been destroyed at Pearl Harbor, the Japanese still held a decided advantage in naval strength and would for some time. The danger was such that Turner had already informed Vandergrift that his transports must be unloaded within two days following the landings. He would risk his fleet no longer. Vandergrift had demanded five, but that, Turner knew, was inviting disaster. Two it would be.

Ordering the naval barrage lifted, Turner watched as the first-wave assault boats formed up, then ploughed toward the smouldering, smoke-drenched Guadalcanal shore. So far, so good, he thought. Still, his feelings of impending doom refused to be calmed.

From the bridge of his flagship, the *Chokai*, Vice Adm. Gunishi Mikawa ordered a course correction to the southeast, then nervously scanned the skies for enemy aircraft. In a few hours his task group would be entering The Slot, the narrow channel running between the upper and lower Solomons. From there, it would be a straight run to the Guadalcanal beachhead where tempting American naval targets were waiting.

Surprise would be essential, he knew. Even though Japanese air controlled the skies, Mikawa worried that a stray reconnaissance plane might sight his hastily assembled fleet, which included five heavy and two light cruisers, plus the destroyer *Yunagi*.

Less than 24 hours before, communications at Rabaul had crackled with word of the American landings on Guadalcanal and several adjacent islands. It had been a surprise. For months, the Army had been saying that no Allied landings could be expected before early 1943. But Mikawa welcomed the opportunity to confront the Americans. Like many senior Japanese naval officers, he still smarted over the ignominious defeat at Midway. Now, the thwarting of America's first attempt at a Pacific offensive was within his grasp. Attacking at night, he would teach these brazen invaders a lesson. For Gunishi Mikawa, revenge would be sweet.

The August 7th Solomons invasion had gone well.

On Guadalcanal, the landings were unopposed, the Japanese having disappeared into the jungle following the naval bombardment. By 1600 on D-Day, a beachhead had been established, the still incomplete airfield taken, and a perimeter established around it. Total marine casualties consisted of one man who had cut his hand attempting to open a coconut with a machete.

In contrast, across Sealark Channel, the northern operations at Tulagi, Gavatu, and Tanambogo had encountered strong enemy opposition.

On Tulagi, Lt. (j.g.) Samuel Miles, a navy doctor serving with Lt. Col. Merritt Edson's 1st Raider Battalion, became the first battle death of the operation.

On the nearby islet of Gavatu, the 1st Parachute Battalion was greeted with heavy small arms fire upon landing. But the determined marines fought to the top of the islet's highest point and by midafternoon had unfurled the American flag.

After a landing attempt by a company of marines was driven off by Tanambogo's defenders, that islet was secured by a battalion of the 2nd Marines after heavy fighting.

Under Adm. Richmond Turner's nervous eye, the transports of Task Force #62 were hastily unloading. But such was the amount of equipment and personnel to be brought ashore that Guadalcanal's beach was soon a jumbled maze of vehicles, ammunition, and other materiel of war.

Meanwhile, to the south, pleading that he was low on fuel, Adm. Fletcher was granted permission to remove his Task Force #61 from the area. The *Wasp*, *Enterprise*, and *Saratoga* sailed off to the east, setting the stage for tragedy.

Shortly after midnight on August 9th, Gunichi Mikawa's naval force slipped into the narrow channel between Savo Island and Guadalcanal. Armed with the new and deadly Long Lance, oxygen-powered torpedoes, Mikawa launched a violent attack against the cruisers and destroyers commanded by Australian Adm. Victor Crutchley. The widely dispersed ships were poorly placed for proper defense. Radar operators had trouble with their new detection equipment. Mikawa's surprise was complete. Within half an hour, his forces had sunk four Allied cruisers and heavily damaged a fifth.

Unaware that Fletcher's carrier group had already left the area, Mikawa chose not to attack Turner's transports standing defenseless off the beach. Instead, with no American force to confront him, he sailed off to the north, having dealt the Guadalcanal invasion fleet a stinging blow.

On shore as a light rain fell, Vandergrift's marines, huddled beneath their ponchos, listened to the rumble of the naval guns, then watched as the sky glowed red from the burning Allied ships.

Just before dawn, as the last of Crutchley's cruisers slipped beneath the waves, darkness once again enveloped the seas off Guadalcanal's shore. Gunichi Mikawa's revenge was complete.

On the morning of August 9th, aboard his flagship, the *Mc Cawley*, Richmond Turner faced the grim fact that his worst fears had been realized. Crutchley's protecting force had been crippled. Added to that, Fletcher's carrier force had left the area, ostensibly to refuel. But Turner knew the real reason for Fletcher's departure. Openly critical of the Guadalcanal operation, he had already lost the *Lexington* and *Yorktown* in earlier naval battles. Fletcher had simply decided not to lose any more carriers.

After confirming Crutchley's losses, Turner felt he had no choice. At noon on August 9th, his transports and cargo vessels, still containing most of the 1st Division's supplies along with thousands of unlanded troops, sailed off to the east. The surviving ships of Crutchley's depleted naval screen followed. Vandergrift and 10,000 of his men were stranded on Guadalcanal. Another 6,000 stood unprotected on Tulagi.

In a stifling command tent just off the airstrip, Gen. Vandergrift, icily calm in the midst of crisis, faced his grim-faced divisional commanders. The situation was critical, he told them. Everything was in short supply. Rations would be cut to two meals a day. Captured Japanese rations and equipment would be utilized. With an enemy counterlanding a growing possibility, Vandergrift ordered the perimeter to dig in, with a focus on the strengthening of beach defenses. Ground action was to be limited to patrols.

Pausing to look through the open tent flap at the rutted, shell-pocked airstrip, evidence of several Japanese air raids, Vandergrift emphasized that completion of the field was crucial. Until he could land combat aircraft, he said, they were all at the mercy of Japanese naval and air power.

The meeting concluded, Vandergrift walked wearily to the communications tent, where he sent a message to the marine commandant in Washington. It ended, "The men are fine, in good spirits and, thank God, still in good health."

At his XVII Army headquarters on Rabaul, Lt. Gen. Harukichi Hyakutake carefully studied a sheaf of intelligence reports just received from the battle area. Scornful of the Imperial Navy's grim reports of a landing in force, Hyakutake believed what Army GHQ in Tokyo told him—that no more than 3,000 low-grade marines occupied the island. Now, without naval cover, they were ripe for the picking. Scanning the list of combat-ready forces at his disposal, the general's eyes settled upon Col. Ichiki's Detachment, a 1,500-man brigade originally slated to occupy Midway Island. Brushing aside painful memories of that disaster, he ordered that the unit, presently stationed on Guam, be dispatched to Guadalcanal with all speed. Hyakutake knew Col. Ichiki by reputation. Ichiki was a resolute, fearless officer who hated westerners with a burning passion—the perfect choice to throw the hated Americans back into the sea.

On August 18th, the airfield on Guadalcanal was ready for use, the final earth having been packed into place by a captured Japanese bulldozer. In a brief but touching ceremony, Gen. Vandergrift named the field for Maj. Loftus Henderson, a marine pilot who had died heroically at the Battle of Midway.

The five-mile marine perimeter now ran from the Tenaru River in the east, through the high ground 1,500 yards south of Henderson Field, to its western boundary at the Matanikau River.

Cautious marine patrols had been making contact with enemy units that were gradually edging closer to the perimeter. Casualties had been taken.

The jungle, too, was taking its toll as malaria and dysentery swept the marine ranks.

On the night of August 18th, a cruiser/destroyer transport force commanded by Rear Adm. Raizo Tanaka landed 815 men of the Ichiki Detachment at Taivu Point on Guadalcanal's eastern shore. It was the first of many reinforcement and resupply runs by Tanaka's force—soon to be dubbed the "Tokyo Express."

Col. Ichiki, spoiling for a fight, was told that the remainder of his brigade—some 700 men—would land within a week. But the feisty Ichiki, convinced that his present strength was sufficient to overwhelm the Americans, marched his men eastward toward the unsuspecting marines.

Thirty-six hours later, as hundreds of Vandergrift's men hooted and howled, two squadrons of American fighter planes from the escort carrier *Long Island* settled down on dusty Henderson Field. Designated MAG #23, the group included 12 Dauntless dive bombers and 19 F4F Wildcat fighters. They were the spearhead of the Cactus Air Force, whose intrepid pilots—often flying aged aircraft held together by glue and baling wire—would soon become the backbone of the island's defense and exact a staggering toll on enemy naval and air groups.

Late that same evening, August 20th, units of the 1st Marines guarding the eastern end of the perimeter heard the distant sound of an approaching enemy. Under the command of Lt. Col. E. A. Pollock, they retired to the western bank of the Tenaru and dug in.

They waited, remembering perhaps a failed attempt by other marine units to eliminate enemy troops west of the Matanikau several days before. Rumor had it that the Japanese encountered in that battle were suicidal—soldiers intent upon dying for their emperor. Now, as Pollock's marines prepared for their initial test in combat, they were grimly determined to accommodate the enemy's wishes.

Ichiki's attack began at 0240, when mortar and cannon fire fell upon Pollock's positions. Two company-strength attacks, with bayonets fixed, followed. The slaughter began. Previously registered marine artillery lobbed deadly accurate fire upon Ichiki's troops. Tanks joined the battle, rolling over the Japanese dead and wounded. Marine machine-gun and rifle fire took a devastating toll. By daybreak, Ichiki's brigade had been cut to pieces. Planes of the newly arrived Cactus Air Force, in low-level strafing attacks over the jungle, finished the job.

Ichiki and a handful of his men who managed to escape stumbled back to Taivu Point. There, after tearing his brigade's colors to shreds, the colonel chose hara-kiri to the unthinkable shame of defeat.

Stunned by Ichiki's disaster, Gen. Hyakutake's determination to retake Guadalcanal became an obsession. He now looked to the 35th Infantry Brigade at Truk, veterans of the fighting in Borneo. The crack unit was led by Maj. Gen. Kiyotaki Kawaguchi.

Despite increasing pressure against Tanaka's "Tokyo Express"—three of his reinforcement-filled destroyers had been sunk by Cactus Air Force planes—Kawaguchi's 4,000-man unit was landed at Taivu Point by the end of August. They moved into the jungle and began hacking a path toward the southern end of Henderson Field. From there, where the high ground was only thinly defended, Kawaguchi would launch his assault.

The field was under constant attack. Night after night, Japanese ships moved in close to pound the strip with high explosives. Exhausted pilots and crews slept fitfully in foxholes and lived on hash, beans, and rice. Still, the Cactus Air Force rose daily to meet the enemy. During one day, its pilots shot down 16 Zeros while losing only four of their own.

Offshore, the naval battles continued. On August 24th, in the Battle of the Eastern Solomons, planes of Adm. Fletcher's task force sank the Japanese light carrier *Ryujo*. One week later, Fletcher's flagship, *Saratoga,* was torpedoed and seriously damaged. Shortly after, the ever-cautious admiral was relieved to pursue other commands.

Amidst reports of an impending Japanese attack, Gen. Vandergrift moved the original Tulagi invasion force—one Raider and one Parachute battalion under Lt. Col. Edson—into the hills south of the airfield. And none too soon.

On the night of September 13th, as 2,000 men of the just-landed Japanese 124th Infantry attacked the marine lines before the Matanikau, Kawaguchi assaulted Edson's positions south of Henderson Field. In a driving rain, his men threw back attack after attack by the frenzied Japanese. Once again, marine artillery exacted a terrible toll. By morning, only mopping up operations remained. Less than 500 of Kawaguchi's men escaped the holocaust. The Battle of Bloody Ridge was history.

Three days later, the 1st Division's 7th Regiment arrived from Samoa to bolster Vandergrift's defenses. By October 7th they had moved into action west of the Matanikau to contest the newly landed Japanese 4th Infantry Division, which was putting extreme pressure on the perimeter. In one ambush, units of the 7th Marines trapped 1,500 enemy soldiers bivouacked in a steep ravine and eliminated them piecemeal.

When intelligence reported an imminent Japanese effort to seize the airfield, the 7th Marines were recalled to the perimeter.

Unknown to Vandergrift, Hyakutake and his XVII Army headquarters had landed in the west on October 9th. By mid-October, Hyakutake commanded a force of 20,000 men. Like Kawaguchi before him, he ordered a road cut through the jungle toward the marine positions.

Amidst a confusion of orders and botched communications, Hyakutake's attack on October 23–24 was doomed from the start. In two days of fierce fighting, Vandergrift's marines, reinforced by the Army's 164th Infantry Brigade, threw back repeated banzai charges. When it was over, there were 3,500 Japanese dead. Hyakutake and his surviving men retreated westward, beyond the Matanikau. The marine perimeter had held.

During the ensuing months, Tanaka's "Tokyo Express" continued landing reinforcements to bolster Hyakutake's presence on the island. But Vandergrift now held the upper hand. On November 14th, when 7 of 11 Japanese transports attempting to land troops were sunk by the Cactus Air Force, Tokyo all but abandoned any hope of retaking Guadalcanal.

Early in December, after four months of grueling combat and more than 2,000 casualties, the 1st Marine Division received word of its relief. On December 9th, after standing in silent prayer at the marine cemetery, Vandergrift passed command to Gen. Alexander M. Patch of the Army's Americal Division.

Subsequently reinforced by the arrival of the 25th Infantry and 2nd Marine divisions, Patch ordered his men to seek out the remnants of Hyakutake's army. The Americans moved out of the perimeter, no longer the hunted—now the hunters.

In the night hours between February 1–2, 1943, 11,000 sick and starving men of Hyakutake's command, all that remained, were taken off the island by Tanaka's ships. Twenty-one thousand Japanese dead were left behind in the tangled silence of the Guadalcanal jungle.

Guadalcanal, Solomon Islands, August 7, 1942. U.S. Marine light tanks move up to lead a patrol.

August 7, 1942. Japanese bombers attack Navy LST's as they prepare to land at Guadalcanal.

U.S. Marines move past dead Japanese defenders. August 8, 1942.

September 13, 1942. "Bloody Ridge," the scene of a fierce battle fought with the Japanese high above the steaming jungles.

The hastily dug grave of a U.S. Marine killed at Lunga Point. September 1942.

September 13, 1942. Exploding Japanese land mines on the Matanikao River.

September 13, 1942. The 35th Infantry Division, 25th Infantry Regiment. A casualty is being placed on a stretcher to be carried to an island hospital.

Evacuating Marine Corps wounded near the Kokumbona River.

A marine position on high ground near "Bloody Ridge." This photograph was taken by marine combat photographer on September 14, 1942.

October 1942. A shattered building frames unloading activities at the reef.

Father Kelly, chaplain of the 2nd Marines, gives aid and solace to the wounded. October 1942.

October 1942. A Navy doctor and a corpsman give a marine aid very close to the action.

U.S. Marines move forward under heavy Japanese fire. October 1942.

November 13, 1942. U.S. Marines carefully close in during the final stages of a battle.

Eight soldiers from the 25th Medical Regiment move a litter up a 50-degree slope under Japanese sniper fire toward an aid station. January 10, 1943.

February 6, 1943. A Japanese soldier killed by BAR fire.

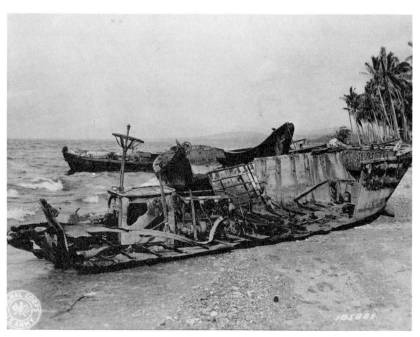

June 9, 1943. Wrecked Japanese landing barges, relics of their occupation of Guadalcanal.

CHAPTER 10 TARAWA: THE KILLING GROUND

"Have landed. Casualties 70%. Can't hold."

—First message from the beach at Tarawa.

Julian C. Smith paused before the meeting-room door to fuss with his tie and tug an extra touch of neatness into his tunic. Eager to get back to war, the 58-year-old major general was only minutes away from finding out where and when.

It was August 1943, and Smith's 2nd Marine Division, blooded in the jungles of Guadalcanal, had spent months reorganizing in the peaceful green countryside outside of Wellington, New Zealand. Now fully recovered from the malaria that had riddled their ranks, they were, like him, anxious to return to the fighting.

Ten minutes later, Smith pored over an invasion map while Vice Adm. Raymond A. Spruance, commander of the 5th Fleet, outlined Operation Galvanic, a two-phase seizure of the Gilbert Islands, 2,000 miles southwest of Pearl Harbor. The landings, a first step in Adm. Nimitz's island-hopping campaign across the Pacific, would be like opening the front door to Japan, Spruance said.

When the admiral pointed out the target, Smith felt a rush of excitement mixed with apprehension. Tarawa atoll, he knew, was one of the most heavily fortified outposts in the Central Pacific. His landing site, Betio, was a tiny islet at the atoll's southwest corner.

Spruance spoke of the "monumental challenges" presented by the campaign. There would be many firsts: the first use of amphibious tractors in carrying troops ashore; the first employment of tanks in an amphibious assault; the first attack by American forces against a defended atoll. D-Day, he announced, would be November 20th.

Moments later, map in hand, Julian Smith strode from the meeting room, eager to tell his marines the good news. They were going back to war.

Three months later, at precisely 5:30 A.M. on a crystal clear morning in the central Pacific, Keiji Shibasaki stepped from his underground command post into the rosy light of a November dawn. The rear admiral, military commander at Tarawa, was anxious to get on with an inspection of some recent additions to Betio's defenses. In the company of several aides, he listened as an animated young naval officer launched into an exhaustive description of the island's formidable fortifications.

Shibasaki was proud of what had been accomplished, pleased that his tiny fortress was ready to meet whatever challenges lay ahead. Honeycombed with pillboxes, bunkers, and concrete blockhouses; ringed with heavy weaponry, including a number of 8-inch cannons that had been "liberated" at Singapore, Shibasaki was convinced that Betio was impregnable. In fact, he had recently boasted to his superiors that the island could not be taken by a million men in a hundred years.

Having toured the southern and western areas, the group

moved along the northern shore, facing the atoll's vast lagoon.

A half-mile out, Shibasaki could see that the coral reef had been exposed by the morning's low tide. The Americans would come from there. They would hit the northern shore and sail straight into his seawall defenses, there to be annihilated by his 4,700 defenders. The admiral smiled. It was a scenario he always found pleasing.

At the islet's eastern tip, the part that narrowed down to a sort of bird's tail, the group paused before a blockhouse as the efficient young officer rambled excitedly about some just-completed concrete reinforcements. As he droned on, Shibasaki's eyes drifted to the eastern horizon. It would soon be dotted with American ships, he knew. Then the hated marines would come. But they were in for a great surprise. Betio was no Guadalcanal. At Betio, Japan would be avenged.

Energized by the thought, Keiji Shibasaki walked on. Time was fleeting and there was still much to be done. The surprised young officer, caught in midsentence, meekly followed with the others.

It began with the big guns. Shortly after 5 A.M. on November 20th, shore batteries on Betio islet opened up on Rear Adm. Harry Hill's invasion fleet. With ear-splitting suddenness, those who had insisted that the Japanese had evacuated Tarawa found themselves wrong.

Guns aboard the American naval vessels standing offshore roared their replies. Among them were the battleships *Maryland* and *Tennessee*, salvaged and modernized after the devastation at Pearl Harbor.

Aboard the *Maryland*, Adm. Hill watched as spiraling smoke and orange fire quickly shrouded the island. "We're going to steamroller that damned place until hell wouldn't have it," he had said. As Betio shuddered from the force of the barrage, it seemed the admiral's promise would be kept.

On the flag bridge, Julian Smith watched as marines of the first wave transferred to the tracked landing boats—or amtracs—that would carry them across the reef and onto the invasion beaches.

The navy's fighters and dive bombers appeared at 0615, a half-hour late, to begin their assault on Betio's 290 acres. Before long, the islet was no longer visible to those offshore. An optimist on the *Maryland*'s bridge proclaimed, "Can't be fifty Japs left alive on that island."

The 42 inbound boats of the assault wave crossed the line of departure. A southeast wind blew smoke directly at them, obscuring the target. The marines crouched low as airbursts exploded above them and bullets from long-range machine guns pinged off their amtracs.

Closer to shore, Lt. Deane Hawkins slowly raised his head above the bow of his landing craft. Fifty yards ahead was Betio's reef. A cold dread seized him. The water, he could see, was barely inches above the coral shelf—too shallow to permit the passage of the flat-bottomed Higgins boats. That meant that only the first-wave amtracs would be able to get across. The rest were in trouble. Damn those tide tables, he thought.

Fifteen minutes ahead of the first wave, Hawkins was leading the 34-man Scout and Sniper Platoon, assigned to neutralize a 500-foot pier bisecting Betio's north shore invasion beaches. From that pier, the Japanese would be able to enfilade the approaching assault waves.

Ten minutes later, at 0855, Hawkins's men, under heavy fire, began their attack. Using grenades, machine guns, and flame throwers, they raced along the decaying pier, blasting the enemy hiding beneath the wood pilings and inside a line of latrines—killing and being killed. Once ashore, Hawkins's men launched an attack against the pillboxes visible above the 4-foot coconut-log seawall. The land battle for Betio islet had begun.

In his Kingfisher observation plane a thousand feet above the island, Lt. Cmdr. Robert A. MacPherson watched the assault waves approach Betio. Something was terribly wrong. While the first-wave amtracs had waddled effortlessly over the reef, the Higgins boats of succeeding waves were bunching up at the coral shelf. Under heavy fire, the marines were abandoning the boats and attempting to wade the 800 yards to shore. MacPherson watched in horror as the men, up to their necks in water, rifles held high, were raked with devastating fire. One after another, helmeted figures slipped beneath the water, never to reemerge. As the carnage unfolded beneath him, MacPherson wanted to cry.

Betio's invasion beaches had been designated—right to left or west to east—Red #1, #2, and #3. The pier that had been assaulted by Hawkins's sniper platoon separated Red #2 and #3.

First wave troops of the 2nd Marine Division reached the smouldering shore under withering fire. At 0910, the 3rd Battalion of the 2nd Regiment—or 3/2—hit Red Beach #1, on the western shore. Seven minutes later, the 2nd Battalion of the 8th Regiment—or 2/8—landed at Red #3 in the east. Moments later, 2/2 went in at Red Beach #2 in the center.

Surprisingly, most of the assault waves landed without heavy casualties. Once ashore, however, the men could only crouch beneath the seawall under murderous fire. Julian Smith's marines quickly realized that Betio was a coral fortress.

On Red Beach #1, Maj. Mike Ryan took command when the battalion commander could not get ashore. Aided by a lone Sherman tank, he rallied the survivors of his three companies and led them off the beach to attack the dug-in Japanese.

On Red #3, Maj. Henry Crowe and his men somehow got two 37mm guns ashore. Wrestling the 900-pound weapons over the seawall, they destroyed one approaching tank and drove off another.

In the center, at Red Beach #2, Col. Herbert Amey, the battalion commander, had been killed in the landing. The survivors of his group were hopelessly pinned down on the narrow beach.

Those ashore looked on in horror as succeeding marines, wading in from the reef, were decimated by the fire from shore. While every instinct told them to remain under cover, groups of marines began hurling themselves at the fortified enemy, desperate to silence the guns wreaking havoc on those trying to land.

Fifteen yards inland from Red Beach #2, in a hole dug behind a still-occupied Japanese pillbox, a wounded Col. David Shoup set up the regimental command post. His radio crackled with "issue in doubt" messages. Desperate calls for naval and air strikes could be heard. Destroyers moved in close to pound the Japanese while carrier planes strafed and bombed the island. These actions, however, did little to diminish the devastating fire coming from Shibasaki's positions.

With nothing able to reach the shore, marine ammunition, food, and water were soon in short supply. Blood plasma was almost gone. Beneath the seawall on Red Beach #3, a 50-yard line of prostrate men awaited attention. Corpsmen and doctors crawled among them, under constant fire. The more seriously wounded were placed in rubber rafts and floated out to the waiting ships. The dead were left unattended, sprawled grotesquely where they had fallen.

On board the *Maryland*, Julian Smith sifted through the grim battle reports. They told him that the operation was at the brink of disaster. Everywhere, the situation was reported as being "extremely critical."

One hundred miles to the north, aboard the battleship *Pennsylvania*, Maj. Gen. Holland M. Smith, commander of Galvanic's amphibious forces, was steeped in his own troubles.

Conducting a joint invasion at Makin Island, the general was enraged at the poor performance of the army's 27th Infantry Division. With more than 6,000 soldiers already landed to contest Makin's 865 defenders, Smith found the army's progress "infuriatingly slow." They would hear about it, he promised himself. He wasn't known as "Howlin' Mad" Smith for nothing.

To add to his troubles, the reports from Tarawa were frightening. Julian Smith's last message had sounded frantic, a request that the reserve 6th Marine Regiment be released to him.

After a quick consultation with Adm. Spruance, Holland Smith sent his approval. He had known Julian Smith for a long time. If the general said he was in trouble—he was in trouble.

By late afternoon, 5,000 marines had been sent to Betio's shore. More than 1,500 of them were already dead or wounded. One company had suffered more deaths in the one day than in their entire stay on Guadalcanal.

But gradually, small groups of men, led by fearless junior officers or noncoms, began leaving the safety of the seawall to fight their way inland. On the eastern and western shores, several tanks joined the action. Bunker after bunker, pillbox after pillbox was silenced by the tanks, demolition teams, and riflemen. Flamethrowers finished the job. Enemy soldiers who tried to flee were shot down. In the fury of the battle, few prisoners were taken.

Betio's sunset was breathtaking. In the midst of the bloodletting, its flaming beauty seemed strangely out of place. Men fighting for their lives paused to take notice—most of them certain it would be their last.

As darkness settled across the island, the embattled marines held two tenuous beachheads. Maj. Ryan's, on the western shore, could be measured in yards. The second, on the northern shore, was 600 yards wide and 250 yards deep, ending at the nearside of the airfield. Between the two beachheads lay another 600 yards of fortified enemy positions. The Japanese also controlled the island's southern shore and its eastern tail.

With the overpowering stench of death everywhere, Smith's marines dug in. Among them Guadalcanal veterans whispered that night always brought banzai charges. This night, they were certain, would be no different. They were wrong.

Adm. Shibasaki watched in frustration as his radio operator tried to raise Japanese units all across Betio. It had been the same since morning. The earth-shattering bombardment preceding the landings had obviously knocked out his communications. Out of touch with his battle commanders, Shibasaki felt impotent. But there was nothing that could be done.

It was maddening. From the few reports that had trickled down to him, the Americans were in desperate trouble. A coordinated night attack would certainly destroy their beach-heads. But how?

The command bunker was unbearably hot. The acrid smells of battle sifted down to Shibasaki and his 300 defenders. He moved among them, urging them on, whispering words of encouragement.

The fighting was getting closer. Without a strong counter-thrust, the Americans would be outside the bunker by morning. But organizing an attack without radio communication was impossible.

Later, as night closed in, the admiral returned to his cramped quarters. It had grown eerily quiet. Only the occasional sound of a mortar round or the chatter of a machine gun could be heard. Shibasaki thought of how nobly his island fortress had endured and how bravely his men had defended it. Then, for the first time, he considered writing down some final, personal thoughts.

At dawn, new tragedy struck. Men of the 1st Battalion, 8th Regiment, who had been waiting offshore in their boats for almost 24 hours, were ordered in. Once again, low water across the reef would not permit passage of the Higgins boats. Few amtracs were available.

Desperately needed by their shipmates ashore, the 8th Marines began wading toward Betio. Murderous fire from the island and from the *Saida Maru*, a Japanese hulk lying offshore, swept their ranks. Only 90 of the first 199 men reached shore.

On Red Beach #1, assisted by naval guns, Mike Ryan continued to clear the western beaches. By midday, elements of the reserve 6th Marines came ashore. Tearfully greeted by Ryan's exhausted men, they moved through their positions and dug in.

At the northern beachhead, Col. Shoup organized a force to fight across the airfield—toward the southern shore. Five enemy machine gun positions stood in the way. The Sniper Platoon's Deane Hawkins, already wounded, volunteered to clean them out. Charging blindly, he destroyed the nests one by one until he was killed by machine gun fire. The fearless Hawkins was awarded a posthumous Congressional Medal of Honor.

By midday, almost unnoticed, the complexion of the battle had changed. More than half of Shibasaki's defenders were already dead. Others, convinced that the fight was lost, began killing themselves in their bunkers. As the marines pushed toward the island's narrowing tail, the cold efficiency of professional soldiers took over. Col. Shoup radioed Julian Smith, "Casualties many—but we are winning."

The third day, November 22nd, began with marine attacks against the enemy pocket in the northwest. The killing was businesslike and brutal. The Japanese resisted furiously, but the end was near.

Julian Smith came ashore on the western beach to greet his weary warriors for the first time. Then, while crossing to the southern shore, his amtrac came under heavy fire and was disabled. Smith transferred to another craft and landed, uninjured, to assume command ashore.

With the marines now in control, the time had come to bury the dead. A trench 3 feet deep by 20 feet long was dredged. The dead, covered with ponchos, were gently laid in the mass grave. As a chaplain intoned the burial rite, a bulldozer pushed dirt over the still forms. These heartrending scenes were replayed over and over.

In his command bunker, Adm. Shibasaki knew the end was near. His last message—which ended *May Japan live for a thousand years*—had been safely stored in a metal strongbox. Outside, the battle was all about him. Some of his men had already taken their lives. Others were running from the bunker, into the gunsights of the Americans. Shibasaki sought to calm those who had remained.

The sound of bulldozers sealing them inside could now be heard. Then the choking smell of gasoline filled the bunker. A muffled explosion was the last sound Keiji Shibasaki heard before a blinding flash enveloped him.

The death spasm of Shibasaki's command occurred on the third night of the battle when hundreds of Japanese emerged from their bunkers to attack the American lines. Methodically, they were cut down by the men of the 2nd Marine Division. By dawn, the carnage had mercifully ended.

The following morning, Holland Smith, having presided over the final moments of the army's plodding campaign at Makin Island, circled the smoking ruins of Betio Islet. The battle was over and Smith could see the terrible price that had been paid.

Later, in the company of Julian Smith, he toured the island, entering the concrete and steel bunkers to stand over Shibasaki's defenders, sprawled next to the heroic marines who had stormed their underground shelters.

Everywhere, Holland Smith saw and heard examples of the incredible heroism displayed by the men. More than 1,000 of them were dead—another 2,000 wounded. In all, 5,500 human beings had perished on the tiny piece of Pacific coral.

But Tarawa, Holland Smith knew, had been a vital testing ground for all the Pacific invasions to come. Mistakes had been made that would never be repeated. Lessons had been learned. Brave marines had died in order to pave the way.

Just before sunset, the two generals stood in silence as a line of dirt-smeared, hollow-eyed marines—young men suddenly grown old—passed by on their way to evacuation boats.

"Howlin' Mad" Smith, always gruff and emotionless, tearfully shook his head. "How did they do it, Julian?" he said, in a voice so low that it was carried off by the gentle breeze blowing across the shattered face of Betio.

Islan. Tense infantry await the order to attack Japanese soldiers. September 13, 1943.

25th Infantry troops land from LCVP's, practicing for the next invasion.

Wildcat fighter pursues Japanese bomber in the Marianas.

Carrier gunners repelling Japan's attack off the Marianas.

A marine with fixed bayonet leads others around a barbed wire entanglement on the beach at Tarawa. September 1943.

Part of assault wave hitting the Bougainville beach. November 1, 1943.

November 14, 1943. U.S. Marines bury their dead during a lull in the fighting.

Bougainville, November 15, 1943. U.S. Marines move toward the enemy.

Bougainville. A captured airstrip is rebuilt and put to immediate use by both Marine and Navy fighters and dive bombers. November 19, 1943.

A marine loaded with hand grenades and extra ammunition takes time out for a drink from his canteen. Tarawa, November, 1943.

Leaders of the Marine Corps assault on Tarawa hold conference in front of bomb-proof command post. Lt. Col. David M. Shoup (center, holding map case) led the assault.

This marine, struck by a piece of shrapnel, gets first aid and a kidding from a corpsman on Tarawa.

Taking aim behind a blasted tree, a marine tries to pick off Japanese soldiers in a distant pillbox.

Japanese Command Post on Tarawa, concrete reinforced with steel, withstood direct hits from artillery fire. On left side of building (beside shadow of tree) is insignia of the Royal Japanese Marines. November 1943.

Lagoon on Tarawa after heavy fighting. Bodies float in the water along with amphibious tractors; one tractor still hangs on the sea wall. November 1943.

Firing slits for three heavy machine guns used by the Japanese can be seen in the log barricade on Betio Island. November 1943.

CHAPTER 11 RETURN TO THE PHILIPPINES

"People of the Philippines. I have returned."

—Douglas MacArthur upon stepping ashore at Leyte.

Douglas MacArthur glanced at his watch, then raised the window shade, hoping for even a fleeting glimpse of Hawaii. Instead, he was greeted by the same layer of fleecy clouds that had covered the Pacific since his plane's departure from New Guinea hours before.

It was July 1944, and the trip was one of the most important of the general's long military career. At Pearl Harbor, he was scheduled to meet with President Roosevelt and Admiral Chester Nimitz to discuss upcoming strategy for the Pacific war.

As head of Southwest Pacific Forces, MacArthur hoped he could avoid an open confrontation with Nimitz, the Navy's Pacific chief. Yet he found himself at serious odds over issues about which he would never compromise.

The war was going well. In France, American forces were set to break out of their Normandy lodgment area. After a difficult stalemate at Cassino, Mark Clark had taken Rome and was again on the move. Nimitz was concluding a successful campaign in the Marianas. And MacArthur's own two-and-a-half-year effort to reclaim the northern coast of New Guinea was ending in total victory.

Now, with the war entering its final stages, he knew that the decisions about to be made at Pearl Harbor were all the more important.

His differences with Nimitz and Fleet Admiral Ernest J. King had arisen over the Navy's strong belief that the Ryukyu Islands and either Formosa or the China coast should be the next major targets in the Pacific war. From these bases, they argued, a final offensive could be mounted against the Japanese home islands. The Philippines, having no real military value, should be by-passed, they said.

MacArthur had been outraged by this final recommendation. His sad and reluctant departure from Corregidor more than two years before had been made only after a solemn promise to return. For the United States to renege on that pledge and sentence the Philippine people to additional months, even years, of brutal enemy occupation was unthinkable. It had become a question of national honor.

King and Nimitz had expressed grave concern over a Philippine campaign. They feared getting bogged down in the islands' vast, impenetrable jungles or becoming involved in costly, time-consuming urban warfare inside the sprawling city of Manila. Beyond that, King had privately argued that MacArthur's seeming obsession with invading the islands was attributable to "sentimental feelings."

Sentiment aside, MacArthur was convinced that a reconquest of the Philippines would provide the best staging area for an invasion of Japan. He was determined to convince President Roosevelt by logic alone.

Sometime later, a glint of sunlight reflecting off the ocean interrupted his reverie. MacArthur looked down and saw that the clouds had parted and the island of Oahu lay dead ahead.

Hurriedly gathering his notes, he thought of Bataan and Corregidor, and of all those he had left behind. Silently, he renewed his pledge not to forsake them.

On the following day, at several meetings held aboard the U.S.S. *Baltimore*, the opposing parties presented their cases to an attentive Franklin Roosevelt.

While Nimitz pressed for landings on Formosa or the coast of China, MacArthur argued that either of these beachheads would be in constant danger from a hostile population. Luzon, he said, protected by the American fleet, would be more suitable for a gathering of forces to make the final assault on Japan.

The President listened to each man, frequently asking probing questions, ultimately reserving judgment.

Although the final decision would not be made for months, MacArthur was confident that he had convinced Roosevelt. As his plane took off for a return to the war zone, the smiling general turned to an aide and said, "We sold it."

The military plan eventually approved called for an invasion of the Palau Islands in September, followed by Philippine landings on Mindanao and Leyte in November and December. Morotai and Ulithi were to be seized as bases to support these operations.

At September's Quebec Conference, the plan was quickly approved by the Combined Chiefs of Staff. But their signatures were hardly dry when the invasion timetable was radically changed.

On August 28th Adm. William Halsey had sallied forth from Eniwetok to conduct fast carrier attacks on Japanese air installations that threatened the Palau and Philippine landings. By September 13th, after his raids had produced little in the way of opposition from the enemy air force, Halsey recommended that the Palau and Mindinao campaigns be scrapped and the Leyte landings moved forward.

While Nimitz insisted that the Palau operation was necessary to secure a fleet anchorage for the Philippine invasion, he agreed to cancel Mindanao and advance the landings at Leyte. An elated MacArthur finalized plans for his long-awaited return.

Following the seizure of Morotai and Ulithi and a bloody marine campaign at Peleliu in the Palaus, 700 ships of Vice Adm. Thomas Kinkaid's invasion fleet approached Leyte. On board were 200,000 men of Lt. Gen. Walter Krueger's VI Army.

In the early morning of October 17th, the armada entered Leyte Gulf to begin a 72-hour search for mines and other obstacles.

At 0943 on the 20th, following naval and air bombardments, the invasion boats, preceded by rocket craft and amphibious tanks, began their run for the beach. On board the flagship *Nashville*, Douglas MacArthur strode the deck, an anxious observer.

Crouched behind the gunwales of their landing craft, Krueger's soldiers were grimly aware that the Japanese defending Leyte were the same men who had taken part in the infamous Bataan Death March.

The landings took place at two points along Leyte's east coast, the beachheads separated by 16 miles.

Maj. Gen. Franklin C. Sibert's 10th Corps, consisting of the 1st Cavalry and 24th divisions, went ashore below Tacloban. Farther south, Maj. Gen. John R. Hodge's 24th Corps landed its 7th and 96th divisions in the area of Dulag.

By late afternoon, Tacloban airfield was in the 1st Cavalry's hands and the 24th had overrun its initial objective, Hill 522.

On Hodge's 24th Corps front, the 96th Division took the high ground and advanced a mile and a half inland while the 7th moved through Dulag and fought its way to the edge of the airstrip.

An impatient MacArthur left the *Nashville* and landed with the third wave near Tacloban. With him was Sergio Osmena, the new president of the Philippines. Flanked by aides, MacArthur waded to shore through knee-deep surf, unsmiling, his jaw set. With Japanese snipers still a threat, he waited as a microphone was set in place. Then, in a Voice of Freedom broadcast heard throughout the islands, he announced his return in a voice trembling with emotion: "By the grace of Almighty God, our forces again stand on Philippine soil—soil consecrated in the blood of our two peoples."

Later, with the area under heavy bombardment, MacArthur sat calmly on a log next to President Osmena. Nearby, American sniper patrols tensely roamed the beach.

As the day wore on, VI Army forces continued to make steady progress against the 16th Division, part of Lt. Gen. Sosaku Suzuki's XXXV Army. By nightfall the navy had put 132,500 men ashore. The reconquest of Leyte was well underway.

On the bridge of his flagship, Vice Adm. Jisaburo Ozawa was furious. Despite every effort, his carrier force, steaming at full speed toward the Philippines, had yet to be discovered by the American navy.

Ozawa's mission was clear cut: to lure Adm. Halsey's Third Fleet away from its defense of the Leyte landings. To accomplish this, Ozawa had gathered about him a squadron of light carriers, battleships converted into carriers, plus cruisers and destroyers. Once his presence was discovered, he would turn north as if to escape. The pugnacious Halsey, unable to resist such inviting targets, would surely follow.

In conjunction with three other fleets, all converging on the Leyte beachhead, Ozawa was part of Operation ShoGo (Victory), a reckless attempt by the Japanese to destroy Adm. Kinkaid's Seventh Fleet and disrupt the Leyte landings.

Once Ozawa had drawn Halsey away from the San Bernadino Straits, which afforded access to the Leyte landing site, separate task forces led by Adms. Kurita and Nishimura were to slip through the straits at night, attack Kinkaid's ships, and destroy the American beachhead.

It was what Halsey didn't know that was critical. Ozawa's task force was only a shell—without significant aircraft and almost no aircrew. Merely a decoy. An irresistible decoy.

After ordering that lengthy messages be broadcast on an open channel to further assure detection, Ozawa settled back to wait. Once the bait was offered, he was confident that the rest would fall nicely into place.

The ensuing Battle of Leyte Gulf became the greatest naval battle in history. Two hundred and forty-four ships took part in the action.

Although Ozawa's decoy fleet was successful in luring Halsey away from the San Bernadino Straits, other American naval forces quickly maneuvered to confront the attacking task groups. In a series of sharp engagements with Kurita, Nishimura, and a third force led by Adm. Shima, they inflicted heavy losses on the enemy.

During these actions, Japanese suicide pilots made their first appearance in force over the American fleet. Although 9 out of 10 were shot from the sky, the kamikaze raids sank several American ships, including the escort carrier, *St. Lo.*

Japan's losses were shattering: 3 battleships, 4 aircraft carriers, 10 cruisers, and 9 destroyers. After Leyte Gulf, the Japanese fleet ceased to exist as an organized force.

On shore, Gen. Suzuki was waging a losing fight. Although his XXXV Army had been reinforced by three divisions from nearby islands, the naval defeat offshore meant that the Philippines were now cut off from outside help. And the American VI Army outnumbered him four to one. Despite the odds, Suzuki was determined to carry on.

By the first week in November, American 10th Corps forces had driven deep into Leyte's northwest valley, overrunning many of its key cities. In the 24th Corps area, Krueger's forces held positions as far south as Abuyog, at the narrow waist of the island. All five of Leyte's airstrips were in VI Army hands. But sluicing autumnal rains had inundated the runways, severely limiting their usefulness.

Elements of the U.S. 77th Division, part of Lt. Gen. Robert Eichelberger's VIII Army, made a December 7th amphibious landing at the west coast port of Deposito. When Ormoc fell three days later, Suzuki could no longer be reinforced. His army was isolated on Leyte.

Although his forces continued to resist furiously, the weight of American arms gradually proved too much. On December 22nd, 10th and 24th Corps troops linked up north of Ormoc. A 77th Division Christmas Day landing at the west coast port of Palompon was the coup de grace. Only futile, suicidal counterattacks by Suzuki's troops remained. By January 4th, Leyte was declared secure.

Having been gradually relieved by VIII Army forces during the final weeks of the Leyte campaign, Krueger's jungle veterans now reboarded their transports for the invasion of Luzon and its prize, the city of Manila.

Early in January 1945, at his jungle headquarters, Lt. Gen. Yamashita finalized plans for the defense of Luzon.

As head of the XIV Area Army, he had commanded some 350,000 men in the Philippines. Now, more than 50,000 of them had been lost on Leyte—thousands more on Mindoro, where the Americans had stormed ashore on December 15th.

Although he had more than a quarter million men on Luzon, most of his units were badly understrength. Added to that, the futile defense of Leyte had seen his available air support whittled down to less than 150 flyable planes.

Yamashita, victor at Singapore, was wise enough to know he could not defend Luzon from shore to shore. Certainly, he would be foolish to contest the Americans on the landing beaches.

In planning his defense, he had broken his army into three groups: The Kembu Group, 30,000 strong, would guard the Bataan Peninsula. The Shimbu Group's 80,000 men had been ordered to defend Manila and the southern part of Luzon. The 150,000 troops of his own Shobu Group would hold out in the inaccessible northern mountains.

Cut off from outside supplies, Yamashita knew that his campaign must end without victory. But he was determined that America would pay dearly for the conquest of Luzon.

At 0930 on January 9th, after an intensive air and naval preparation, assault forces of Krueger's VI Army began landing on the picture-perfect beaches of Lingayen Gulf, 100 miles north of Manila. There was no opposition.

The invasion point, midway up Luzon's west coast, led directly to the central plain, thence to Manila. The same landing site had been successfully used by the Japanese in their December 1941 invasion of the island.

As Douglas MacArthur came ashore to pose for photographers, spearhead units pushed inland. By nightfall the beachhead was 17 miles wide and 4 miles deep.

Maj. Gen. Oscar Griswold's 14th Corps, made up of the 37th and 40th Infantry Divisions, pushed into the central plain toward Manila.

On their left, Maj. Gen. Innis Swift's 1st Corps advanced alongside, ordered to protect Griswold's flank from an attack from the north.

Facing Yamashita's powerful Shobu Group, Swift found that the Japanese were well entrenched along a 25-mile chain of strong points from Lingayen to the Cabaruan Hills. As a consequence, his advance was painfully slow.

Pushing toward Manila against scant opposition, Griswold was fearful of getting too far ahead of the plodding Swift, thereby exposing his left flank. As a result, the entire American advance moved forward at a snail's pace.

MacArthur quickly intervened, stressing the urgency of reaching Manila as soon as possible. Not only was the port badly needed, he said, but thousands of civilian and military prisoners who had been held in brutal captivity since the early days of 1942 were awaiting liberation.

Despite the general's exhortations, the reinforced 1st Corps took until late January to force Yamashita into the mountains of northern Luzon. Finally, after a violent tank battle, Swift drove rapidly to the eastern shore. Yamashita was now cut off from his forces in the center and south of the island.

Slowed by Swift's heavily contested advance, Oscar Griswold's 14th Corps finally pushed the Kembu Group back beyond Clark Field. The assault on Manila was rapidly taking shape.

On January 29th, the 11th Corps' 38th Infantry Division made an amphibious landing near San Antonio, close to the Bataan Peninsula. Fearful of seeing his forces trapped there—as MacArthur's had been in 1942—Yamashita ordered most of his combat units to withdraw.

Three days later, the VIII Army landed 8,000 men of the 11th Airborne Division near Nasugbu, 50 miles southwest of Manila. They immediately began a rapid advance, reaching the city's outskirts on February 4th. When elements of the 1st Cavalry Division broke into Manila from the north, the battle for the "Pearl of the Orient" was joined.

At his command post inside the city, Rear Adm. Sanji Iwabuchi planned for a last-man defense of the capital. As the commander of 17,000 picked naval forces, he was responsible to no one. Yamashita, who would have chosen not to defend Manila, was trapped in the north and powerless to stop him. Iwabuchi was adamant. The city would yield only after every member of his naval brigade was dead.

Splitting his forces into three battle groups, he urged his commanders to stand firm.

Weeks of savage fighting ensued. But the diehard sailors were gradually forced to take refuge in the old walled city of Intramuros.

Iwabuchi's refusal to pass civilians through his lines resulted in horrendous casualties among Manila's citizens. The need to blast his fanatical defenders from their fortified positions saw the city's buildings crumble, one by one. Fires raged day and night.

Amidst the smoke and ruin, the first of Manila's prison camps was liberated. After three years of despair, the combat veterans of Bataan and Corregidor were free. With them were the brave army nurses who had shared their torturous confinement.

Visiting the camps, Douglas MacArthur emotionally greeted old friends. "I'm sorry I took so long getting back," he said.

The walls of Intramuros were finally breached and VI Army forces stormed in to destroy what was left of Iwabuchi's brigade. The brutalized civilian population streamed out. Everywhere, the human suffering was beyond belief.

On March 2nd the last organized resistance inside Manila collapsed. The city lay in ruins, a more complete picture of destruction than London or Warsaw.

That same day, three years after his hasty departure, MacArthur returned to Corregidor. The island fortress had been reclaimed by army parachutists after a bitter 10-day struggle.

Seeing the old flagpole still standing, MacArthur said to the commanding officer, "Have your troops hoist the colors to its peak—and let no enemy ever haul them down again."

As the flag was slowly raised to the playing of The Star-Spangled Banner, the general stood at attention, crisply saluting, his happy eyes brimming with tears. For one old soldier, a long-ago promise had been fulfilled.

Bataan, May 1942. The Death March. Taken during the march from Bataan to Cabana Tuan Prison Camp.

Japanese photograph of civilian internees on Santo Tomas in the Philippines. Taken in May 1942.

March 1942. A Japanese photograph of U.S. prisoners in the Philippines.

January 2, 1944. 126th Infantry Regiment of the 32nd Division rushes from landing craft during the invasion at Saidor, New Guinea.

Kwajalein, February 1, 1944. 7th Division soldiers set up radio in a bomb crater near Red Beach to direct artillery fire.

Eniwetok Atoll, Marshall Islands, February 17, 1944. U.S. Marines cover an advancing patrol looking for Japanese snipers.

Admirals Spruance, Sherman, Nimitz, and Marine General Vandergrift review war plans on Guam.

February 19, 1944. Marines set up communications on the beach of Eniwetok Atoll.

Eniwetok Atoll, February 20, 1944. Heavy Naval shelling destroyed Japanese planes before they could take off.

Eniwetok Atoll, February 21, 1944. Marine units rest before moving up to engage the Japanese.

February 28, 1944. General of the Army Douglas MacArthur observes the shelling of Los Negros from the bridge of the USS *Phoenix*. With him are Vice Admiral Thomas C. Kinkaid and Colonel Lloyd LaHrbas, General MacArthur's aide.

Bougainville, March 1, 1944. 93rd Infantry Division troops advance warily in Kunai grass.

Brisbane, Australia, March 27, 1944. General Douglas MacArthur, commander-in-chief, South West Pacific Area, explains his strategy to Admiral Chester M. Nimitz, commander-in-chief, Pacific Fleet.

Burma (China Burma India) Theatre. Brigadier General Frank Merrill, commander of Merrill's Marauders, reports to General Joseph W. Stillwell on China operations. March 1944.

Merrill's Marauders mule skinners clean their rifles on a forced march somewhere in Burman jungle.

Bougainville, April 1, 1944. Troops of the 148th Infantry of the 32nd Division behind the wedge of advancing tanks of the 754th Tank Battalion.

New Guinea, May 18, 1944. First and second waves of the 41st Division are pinned down by Japanese machine-gun fire. These men are from the 163rd Infantry Regiment.

June 17, 1944. First U.S. casualty on Saipan, hit by a Japanese sniper. He is being carried by litter-bearer medics.

Tanapag Harbor, Saipan, July 6, 1944. Dead Japanese soldiers litter the beach after a counterattack against U.S. Marines.

Tokyo is the target of Admiral Chester Nimitz's pointer. Present at the plans briefing are President Franklin D. Roosevelt, General Douglas MacArthur, and Admiral William Leahy. The photograph was taken on July 27, 1944.

September 15, 1944. 1st Marine Division units dot the ridges of Peleliu after routing the Japanese defenders.

September 15, 1944. 1st Marine Division light machine gun covers the beach during landings at Peleliu.

1st Marine Division officers and noncoms are briefed before the invasion begins. September 15, 1944.

Peleliu, September 15, 1944. Heavy enemy small-arms fire pins the marines on the beach. 1st Marine Division units start to move up the ridge.

September 17, 1944. 1st Marine Division unit guides a wounded marine down from the bloody ridges of Peleliu.

September 20, 1944. Medium tanks take a vital airfield on Peleliu.

Palau Operation, September 20, 1944. 81st Division troops, supported by their tanks, captured the island of Anguur after bitter fighting.

Palau Operation, September 21, 1944. The 81st Division took the island after hard fighting. Their ammunition dump hit, firefighters are trying to extinguish the blaze.

September 21, 1944. 81st Division 4.2 chemical mortars clean out the last of the Japanese installation in Palau. The fighting had been intense.

Assault troops head for the Leyte Beach.

General MacArthur and Major General Mudge on Leyte. October 21, 1944.

A 24th Division chaplain holds Mass for Americans and Filipinos. October 22, 1944.

Leyte Gulf, 1944. A Japanese aircraft carrier wallows in distress off Leyte, Philippine Islands.

Leyte Island, Philippines, December 11, 1944. An 81mm-mortar squad fires on counterattacking Japanese at Ormoc, near the Antilse River. December 11, 1944.

Luzon, Philippine Islands, January 25, 1945. Bill Schlacki entered the service from Buffalo, N.Y. Here he fires a flamethrower at a Japanese machine-gun emplacement.

Luzon, January 27, 1945. GI's cover the advance of a flamethrowing unit getting into position to burn out an enemy pillbox.

U.S. soldiers move up to wipe out a Japanese pillbox that has already killed one of them. January 30, 1945.

A Japanese 12-inch gun captured in Luzon by troops of the 43rd Infantry Division. GI's examine their prize. February 4, 1945.

February 4, 1945. Manila burns: The Japanese set dynamite charges at key locations.

Manila, February 5, 1945. Elements of the 2nd Battalion, 5th Cavalry Regiment, approach Rizal Memorial Stadium, where Japanese soldiers are well hidden on the perimeter of the grandstand.

Corregidor, Philippines. Paratroopers of the 503rd Parachute Infantry land on February 16, 1945.

Corregidor. Pfc. Lyle O. Slaght of the 503rd Parachute Infantry Regiment (right).

February 17, 1945. These three Japanese soldiers were killed by a white phosphorus grenade during the battle to retake Corregidor.

February 23, 1945. Infantrymen return fire from Japanese positions in the Intramuros section of Manila.

February 23, 1945. Soldiers climb across the breached wall of Intramuros.

February 23, 1945. A flamethrower kills the last of the Japanese soldiers hiding in the wall that surrounds Manila's inner city.

Corregidor, March 7, 1945. A Japanese suicide squad is stopped by infantrymen prepared to meet them head-on.

Cebu Island, Philippines, March 26, 1945. The first troops crawl ashore. The first to land was the 2nd Battalion, 132nd Infantry, of the Americal Division. They are under heavy Japanese small-arms fire in this surprise landing.

Cebu Island, March 26, 1945. With the 2nd Battalion ashore, the 3rd Battalion of the 132nd Infantry wades toward shore.

Luzon, April 26, 1945. T/4 Harry Myers of Middletown, N.Y., a member of the 775th Tank Battalion of the 37th Division, helps a woman refugee up a steep slope near the city of Baguio.

GI's of the 152nd Infantry Regiment keep low as a satchel charge explodes in a Japanese dugout. This took place in Rizal Province, Luzon, on May 22, 1945.

May 28, 1945. Three infantrymen from A Company, 149th Regimental Combat Team, 38th Division, cover an advancing patrol on a narrow road near the Tawa Dam, Luzon.

Luzon, June 5, 1945. 1st Infantry Regiment troops advance against Japanese positions on Cabaruan Hill. They are under the cover of a smoke screen.

Luzon, June 5, 1945. 129th Regiment troops attack Japanese soldiers hiding in a culvert by throwing phosphorus grenades. This incident took place near Aritao.

Manila. U.S. troops walk by a Japanese soldier killed by a flamethrower.

Manila. U.S. antitank troops fire 37mm shells at a Japanese machine-gun nest in a church tower at the end of the street. The photograph was taken on June 18, 1945.

Luzon. In an attempt to infiltrate the perimeter of Battery A, 139th Field Artillery, this Japanese soldier was shot. He still holds a U.S. hand grenade. This photograph was taken on July 20, 1945.

Manila. The Japanese soldier still hangs on the frame of a truck that was ambushed by GI's.

Allied prisoners are freed from Aomori Compound. They hail their deliverers. July 1945.

These are liberated U.S. prisoners after three years in Bilbid Prison. July 1945.

12 OKINAWA: THE LAST BATTLE

"I realize now that we are all doomed."

—Entry in Japanese diary following Okinawa landings.

Shortly after daybreak on April 1, 1945, the roar of naval guns jolted the Easter Sunday silence.

Several miles off the southeast coast of Okinawa, an island less than 400 miles from Japan, final preparations for an amphibious invasion commenced.

Assault troops of the 2nd Marine Division clambered down transport cargo nets and into the assault boats.

Wave after wave of carrier-based aircraft began strafing the landing ground and pounding the inland hills with rockets.

By 0800, marine-filled amtracs had formed into eight attack waves that stretched endlessly along the smoke-shrouded beach. With amphibious tanks leading the way, the unwavering lines of LVT's ploughed shoreward with all the precision of a peacetime rehearsal.

On board the flagship, Maj. Gen. Thomas E. Watson, the marine commander, watched as the first wave approached the burning shore. It was 0829.

Seconds later, an incredible scene developed. As though on signal, the hundreds of landing craft executed neat 180-degree turns and began moving away from the beach. Within half an hour, the assault troops were back on board their transports and the invasion fleet was retiring seaward.

On the flagship, Gen. Watson congratulated all hands. Then he hurried below for news of the real invasion on Okinawa's western shore, 25 miles to the northwest. His own operation had been nothing more than a feint.

Operation Iceberg, the invasion of the Ryukyus, had been born out of bitter dispute.

Douglas MacArthur had recommended that it be bypassed, its garrison left to "wither on the vine." America's naval chief, Adm. Ernest J. King, had favored an invasion of Formosa. Only Adm. Nimitz, head of Central Pacific Forces, had pressed for the seizure of Okinawa as a firm base for the upcoming invasion of Japan.

The island, 60 miles long and 2 to 18 miles wide, was the merging point of Nimitz and MacArthur's two-pronged, island-hopping offensive that had started two years before. It would place the Allies within the inner ring of Japan's defenses. And, given the increasing ferocity of Japanese resistance as the war neared the home islands, it promised to be the most fierce and bloody battle of the Pacific war to date.

Aerial reconnaissance had revealed that the principal Japanese defenses were located at the southern half of the island, just below its narrow waist. Okinawa's limestone foundation favored the construction of deep bunkers like those utilized with such lethal effect in recent operations. The campaign promised to be a carbon copy of Iwo Jima—with the Japanese yielding the beaches to draw the American invaders inland, out of range of naval gunfire, toward the heavily fortified positions.

Naval intelligence had reported that the island was garrisoned by 70,000 troops of Lt. Gen. Mitsuru Ushijima's XXXII Army. An additional 27,000 men—naval forces and armed workers—were also available. The overpopulated island, mountainous and rugged in the north, with terraced farmland dominating the south, was also home to 450,000 civilians.

On that cool, clear April 1st, with a light breeze sweeping across the East China Sea, Adm. Raymond Spruance's Fifth Fleet gathered off Okinawa's western shore, facing the Hagushi beaches. Dotting the horizon beneath low-lying clouds, it was the largest amphibious force ever assembled—300 warships and 1,139 auxiliary vessels.

On board were 180,000 men of Lt. Gen. Simon Bolivar Buckner's X Army—consisting of two marine and four infantry divisions. Including support services, the invasion force involved almost a half million men.

The naval barrage was augmented by long guns from outlying islands that had been seized during the prior week. Fleet anchorage positions had also been secured on the Kerama Rhetto Islands, 20 miles to the west.

Since Okinawa was within easy range of Japanese airfields on Formosa and Japan, fast carrier attacks had been instituted against those installations for a week preceding the invasion. During these assaults, Adm. Halsey's ships had fallen victim to Japanese kamikazes that appeared in force. The carriers *Saratoga*, *Franklin*, and *Wasp* had been badly mauled and were out of action. But Halsey's efforts had been successful. On invasion day, few enemy planes were seen over Spruance's fleet.

At 0832, the first Americans touched the Okinawa shore. Aside from inaccurate mortar fire coming from the bluffs behind the beach, the landings were unopposed.

Maj. Gen. Roy C. Geiger's 3rd Amphibious Corps, consisting of the 1st and 6th Marine divisions, landed on the left. The 6th was to capture Yontan airfield, then cut northeast, toward the Ishikawa Peninsula. The 1st was to drive for the Katchin Peninsula on the island's east coast.

Maj. Gen. John R. Hodge's 24th Corps, consisting of the 7th and 96th Infantry divisions, landed on the right. While the 7th seized Kadena airfield and dashed for the east coast, the 96th was ordered to take the high ground commanding the beaches, then turn right, toward the southern end of Okinawa.

With the Japanese nowhere to be seen, Buckner's X Army troops moved rapidly inland. Spirits rose. A beaming infantryman standing on a hill overlooking the beach expressed the growing optimism felt by all. "I've already lived longer than I thought I would," he said.

In the first hour, 16,000 men were landed. Both airfields fell before sunset. By nightfall, with 60,000 men ashore, the beachhead was 9 miles wide and 2 to 3 miles deep. In some places, Buckner's troops were within sight of the eastern shore. The landings had been picture-perfect—the most successful of the three-year Pacific war. But the real battle was still to begin.

Just after sunrise on April 6th, as the battleship *Yamato* cleared the Van Diemen Straits, Vice Adm. Seiichi Ito ordered a change of course to the west. Within seconds, the monstrous warship gracefully responded, turning easily away from the bright morning sun. The cruiser *Yahagi* and eight destroyers escorting the Japanese behemoth followed suit.

On the previous day, Ito had departed Tokuyama, on Japan's

inland sea, negotiating the difficult Bungo Strait at night. Now, he would sail due west for several hours—out of range of American search planes—before making a southward turn for Okinawa to lead his final battle.

Without air cover, Ito knew there was no hope that he would ever return to his beloved homeland. But his mission was clear: to steam directly to the Okinawan beachhead and sink any American ships that might have survived the mass kamikaze raid even now attacking the invasion fleet. With only enough fuel for a one-way trip, Ito would then beach the giant 863-foot *Yamato* and order its crew of 2,767 officers and men to debark and fight ashore.

Ito was proud that he had been chosen to lead the mission, one that would cap his long and honorable naval career. The *Yamato*, he knew, was superior in firepower to anything the Americans had afloat. With her nine 18.1-inch guns boasting a range of more than 22 miles, he was confident that his tiny task force would take its toll on the American fleet before the end came.

Ito thought of the hundreds of kamikaze pilots who were, at that very moment, dying gloriously for their emperor. He prayed for the strength to complete his mission and for the honor of joining them in their sacred reward.

As he sailed westward, Ito's every movement was known to the American fleet. On the previous evening, two U.S. submarines, *Threadfin* and *Hackleback*, had reported the *Yamato's* position as she sailed through the Bungo Straits.

Aboard the carrier *Bunker Hill*, Adm. Marc Mitscher now waited impatiently. When advised of the sighting the night before, he had moved his task force to the north, positioning it for a quick strike. Mitscher wanted the *Yamato* with a vengeance. His concern was that Adm. Spruance might order the fleet's battleships to engage the Japanese giant. As soon as the *Yamato* turned toward Okinawa, he was ready to attack. Then he could only pray that Spruance wouldn't countermand his action.

At 0823 on April 7th, as Ito turned south for his dash to the Okinawan beachhead, the *Yamato* was sighted by one of Mitscher's carrier planes. The admiral was notified. While a high-flying navy patrol bomber and the two submarines shadowed Ito's battle group, Mitscher's prepared to launch planes.

Shortly before 12:30, with the *Yamato* still 250 miles from Okinawa, spotters aboard the battleship reported the approach of enemy aircraft. Moments later, attacking through heavy rain squalls, Mitscher's dive bombers and torpedo planes scored their first hit on the huge ship. Three bombs struck forward of the great stern turret while three torpedoes smashed in the *Yamato's* hull. By the time Mitscher's second-wave strike force appeared, Ito's ship was listing badly.

For two hours, the *Yamato* and her escort ships absorbed a ferocious pounding from the American carrier planes. At 1400, the cruiser *Yahagi* went down. Twenty-three minutes later, Mitscher had his prize. The *Yamato* capsized and slid beneath the East China Sea, joining her sister ship, the *Musashi*, lost at Leyte Gulf. Ito and most of his crew died with her. Four of the eight escorting destroyers were also sunk. The others limped northward.

The loss of the *Yamato* signaled the end of the great battleships' mastery of the seas. With the navy's task groups now built around the aircraft carrier, the big-gunned capital ships, no longer the spearhead of naval action, were relegated to little more than escort duty. Not another battleship has ever been built. With the demise of the *Yamato*, the centuries-long reign of the dreadnought sadly ended.

At the Okinawa beachhead, ships of Spruance's invasion fleet were caught in the first stages of Operation Ten-Go, a series of 10 deadly kamikaze raids that began on April 6th and lasted, intermittently, until June 22nd. These mass attacks, known as *kikusui* (floating chrysanthemum) raids, inflicted terrible damage on the American fleet. Twenty-one ships were sunk and 66 others severely damaged.

Particularly hard hit were ships on the radar picket line, a group of destroyers and other vessels disposed around Okinawa from 15 to 100 miles from land. They were intended to pick up approaching aircraft on radar, then notify the combat air patrol to intercept. The kamikazes quickly zeroed in on these sentries. Their casualties comprised a great percentage of the 4,900 sailors killed during the Okinawa fighting.

On shore, the land campaign that had begun so quietly was rapidly developing into a full-fledged battle.

In the first days, marine and army units had slashed across to Okinawa's eastern shore, cutting the island in two. As ordered, the 6th Marine division then turned northeast, to clean out the mountainous regions of the Motobu Peninsula. After a four-day, 20-mile advance, they came up against a well-organized defense system in an area of rocky ridges known as the Yae Take. There, 2,500 deeply entrenched Japanese soldiers had to be eliminated.

At the same time, the 6th Division's 22nd Regiment swept the rugged northern tip of the island.

While the 1st Marine Division was engaged in sharp fighting with guerilla-type units, the 24th Corps turned south to meet the first well-organized enemy resistance.

Beginning just above the capital at Naha and running to the southern tip of the island, Ushijima had constructed a powerful three-ring line of east-west defenses, each ring honeycombed with mutually supporting bunkers, pillboxes with steel doors impervious to flamethrowers, and a maze of interconnected trenches.

At the first of these rings, known as the Machinato Line, the 24th Corps was locked in a violent struggle to uproot the dug-in enemy. Persistent attacks against a position known as Kakazu Ridge failed to breach the Japanese line. By April 12th, all along the Machinato front, the 24th Corps had been brought to a halt.

On that day, America's fighting men despaired as word of the death of President Franklin D. Roosevelt quickly spread. "What will happen to us now?" was heard, over and over. Soldiers, sailors, and airmen paused to mourn their wartime leader and wonder silently about his successor, Harry S. Truman.

On April 9th, Gen. Buckner landed his reserve 27th Division and sent them south in an attempt to break the stalemate. They moved into the right side of the line, prepared to attack.

The Japanese struck first. In a move contrary to his battle plan, Ushijima launched his 24th and 62nd divisions in a surprise counterattack. When repeated assaults over a two-day period were repelled with heavy losses, the Japanese commander recalled his forces and returned to the defensive.

A lull fell over the battlefield.

On April 16th, having decided that the airfields on Ie Shima, a small island off Okinawa's northwest coast, would be useful to support his land battle, Buckner sent the 77th Division ashore. All three airfields and the western half of the island fell on the first day. But the Japanese resisted tenaciously in Ie Town and bitter fighting ensued before the island was secured on April 24th.

In the Ie Shima fighting, America lost its premier war correspondent, killed by a Japanese sniper while closely following the assault units. Grieving GI's erected a simple sign reading AT THIS SPOT, THE 77TH DIVISION LOST A BUDDY, ERNIE PYLE.

On April 19th, Buckner threw the 27th Division against Kakazu Ridge. Efforts to slip around Ushijima's strongpoints were sharply contested. Said one frustrated officer, "You cannot bypass a Jap because a Jap does not know when he is bypassed." Once again, the formidable enemy defenses failed to yield.

Unable to crack through in the center, an impatient Buckner now launched a series of determined assaults against both ends of Ushijima's line. Gradually, the Japanese flanks were bent back, threatening the center with envelopment. Finally, on April 24th, the Machinato Line was pierced and Buckner's soldiers moved through for what proved to be a brief advance.

Four days later, they came up against the main point of Ushijima's defenses, a line of fortifications built around Shuri Castle. The area, one of rugged hills, defiles, and deep caves, was dominated by the castle, an ancient dwelling where the kings of Okinawa had reigned. In 1853, at a nearby hill called The Pinnacle, Commodore Matthew Perry had raised the American flag to the cheers of his men. Now it became the scene of fierce fighting that would test the resolve of the Americans as never before.

With the northern part of Okinawa secured, Buckner moved the 1st Marine Division into the right of the line to relieve the battered 27th. At the same time, the 77th took over for the casualty-ridden 96th. Right to left, Buckner's line now consisted of the 1st Marine Division, the 77th and 7th Infantry divisions.

As seasonal "plum rains" deluged the island, turning Okinawa into a huge quagmire, the front quieted. Plans were made for a final offensive aimed at breaking through Ushijima's Shuri fortifications.

Before Buckner could strike, the desperate Japanese launched their own attack.

It began with a devastating kamikaze raid on American ships anchored offshore. Several were sent to the bottom. Then, in the early hours of May 4th, Japanese infantry began a three-pronged assault against the center and right of the X Army line. Although an enemy attempt to land amphibious troops behind the American line was sighted and annihilated, deep penetrations were made against the 7th and 77th divisions. When Tanaburu and Tanaburu Ridge fell, the situation turned critical. Leaving the weary 27th to clean up the north, Buckner moved the 6th Marine Division into the right of the line, the 1st sliding left. It had now become a two corps front—the 24th on the left, the 3rd on the right.

As the Americans struggled to retake the lost ground, word was received that Germany had surrendered. Said one American colonel while picking away with his rifle, "Now if we can just get those damn Japs off that ridge, everything'll be fine, won't it?"

Buckner's offensive kicked off on May 11th with the 6th Marine Division moving toward Naha, the Okinawan capital.

The 1st Marines attacked Shuri fortifications at places called Dakeshi Ridge and Wana Draw. On the right, the 24th was involved at Ishimmi Ridge and Conical Hill.

The fighting seesawed back and forth for more than a week. On the 19th, critical Sugar Loaf Hill was taken, followed by Conical Hill two days later. Naha fell on the 23rd. Ushijima's line was finally cracking.

In his command post, far beneath Shuri Castle, the Japanese commander made the painful decision to withdraw to his final defense line. While a rear guard held off Buckner's forces, long lines of Japanese began streaming south. For the moment, overcast skies and constant rain protected them from the eyes of American airmen.

On May 29th, the 5th Marines entered the ruins of Shuri Castle. From the rubble, an ancient, shell-scarred bronze bell was unearthed. An inscription read, *The bell will echo far and wide—like a peal of thunder—and evil men, hearing it, will be saved.*

Clearing weather saw American planes initiate violent attacks against Ushijima's retreating columns as they moved south for a final stand. Losses were heavy. The exhausted survivors straggled into their new positions southeast of the Oroku Peninsula.

For three weeks in June, this final line became the scene of the bloodiest fighting of the campaign.

A naval force under Rear-Adm. Minoru Ota was cleaned out of the Oroku with the help of a 6th Marine Division amphibious landing.

Ushijima's defenders fought with a fury unequalled in the long battle. The 8th Marines of the 2nd Division were rushed from Saipan to join the fight. Gradually, the Japanese defense began to buckle. The strongpoint at Kunishi Ridge yielded to the 7th Marines. Fortified caves on Mount Yuza and Mount Yaeju were the last to fall. As the Japanese became a desperate mob, the remaining few pockets of resistance were eliminated. Hundreds of enemy soldiers, refusing to surrender, blew themselves up with hand grenades or satchel charges. Others hurled themselves from the steep Okinawan cliffs.

On June 18th, while visiting a forward command post, Gen. Buckner was killed by shrapnel from a Japanese artillery shell. Gen. Geiger assumed command, thus becoming the first marine officer to lead an American army.

All resistance on Okinawa ended on June 21st. In the early hours of the following morning, at his own order, Gen. Ushijima was beheaded by an adjutant.

The bitter fight for Okinawa—which has been called an epic of human endurance—had been won at a terrible price. Fifty thousand Americans were dead, wounded, or missing. The Japanese had lost 110,000 soldiers and airmen.

The way to Japan was now open. But the invasion of the home islands, set for November 1, 1945, never took place. Events already in progress soon combined to make the bloody struggle for Okinawa the last battle of World War II.

Mort Zimmerman, U.S. Coast Guard Signalman Second Class, handling ship-to-shore communications in Buckner Bay. March 26, 1945.

Kerrama Rhetto, March 26, 1945. A unit of the 77th Infantry Division takes shelter behind a sea wall before advancing into Zamami Shima.

March 26, 1945. 77th Division soldiers carry a load of rations and ammunition up a steep slope at Tokashiki Shima.

March 31, 1945. 77th Division soldiers raise the American flag over a Japanese home island at Geruma Shima. It is the first time this has ever happened.

April 1945. Alligators leave LSTs and head for Ie Shima.

Ie Shima, April 20, 1945. This Japanese soldier was part of a counterattacking unit that attempted to attack the U.S. Tenth Army.

April 1945. 77th Division veteran infantry-man runs past a burning building at Ie Shima. The great war reporter and author, the legendary Ernie Pyle, was killed by a sniper's bullet near here.

April 1945. More 77th Infantry Division troops leave LCIs and LCMs.

April 1945. 2nd Division Marines landed by Coast Guard at Iheya Shima.

April 1945. 7th Division infantrymen head for the Okinawa bridgehead.

Infantrymen use riflefire grenades and BAR fire to dislodge Japanese soldiers from their caves. This photograph was taken on April 20, 1945.

May 11, 1945. An M-18 tank of the 306th Antitank Company fires at the enemy at Shuri.

May 15, 1945. A U.S. tank blasts enemy strong points with a flamethrower. The Japanese are holed up in a series of interconnected caves.

June 17, 1945. The 713th Flamethrowing Armored Regiment shells Japanese positions on Coral Ridge. Troops find safety behind the tank and an outcrop.

June 20, 1945. Soldiers of L Company, 383rd Infantry Regiment, are exhausted after an intense battle for "Big Apple Hill."

The minesweeper *Lindsey* took two kamikazes off Okinawa and still remained afloat. The bow forward of the bridge has been sheared, leaving a wilderness of twisted metal and pipes.

August 12, 1945. The USS *Pennsylvania*, a battleship, suffered a very dangerous aerial torpedo hit by Japanese aircraft off Okinawa. Only skilled repairs and determination saved the ship.

The cruiser USS *Birmingham* is ripped by a kamikaze hit off Okinawa. August 1945.

The aircraft carrier *Bunker Hill* is screened by two destroyers after suffering a kamikaze attack.

The hangar deck of the USS *Bunker Hill*, the result of kamikaze hits by two planes.

The USS *William D. Porter*, sinking after a suicide attack by Japanese "Divine Wind" aircraft.

CHAPTER 13 HIROSHIMA: THE FINAL AGONY

"My God! What have we done?"

—Co-pilot of the *Enola Gay* watching mushroom cloud over Hiroshima.

At 0245 on August 6, 1945, Col. Paul W. Tibbets, Jr., advanced the throttles of his B-29, *Enola Gay,* to full power. Grudgingly, the big bomber, part of the 509th Composite Group, started down the runway at Tinian Island's North Field in the Pacific Marianas.

The takeoff speed increased with numbing slowness. Tibbets watched as the emergency equipment positioned along the runway flashed by. So did the burned-out hulks of B-29's that had failed to negotiate recent takeoffs—one on the preceding day.

Co-pilot Robert Lewis called out the ground speed in a voice tight with tension. The 10,000-foot strip—one of four—was more than adequate for the takeoff of a B-29 carrying a normal load. But Tibbets's plane was 15,000 pounds overweight. Both he and Lewis knew it would be close.

With less than 1,000 feet left, Lewis found his hands instinctively reaching for the yoke. "No! Leave it," Tibbets snapped, eyes glued to the spot where the runway lights ended. Seconds later, he eased back on the controls. For what seemed an eternity, nothing happened. Then, the "Superfortress" shuddered into the air at the same instant that the runway beneath it was replaced by the blackness of the Pacific.

Leveling out at 4,700 feet, Tibbets set a north-by-northwest course for Iwo Jima, 650 miles distant. The 509th's Special Bombing Mission #13 was on its way.

For Tibbets, a combat veteran of North Africa and Europe, it was a very special assignment. Firmly secured in the plane's enlarged bomb bay was the world's first uranium bomb. In five hours, he would unleash its awesome power on Japan. The mission, if successful, could bring a rapid end to the war.

Due to concerns about a takeoff crash, it had been decided to arm the weapon in flight. As the *Enola Gay*—named for Tibbets's mother—cruised through the clear night sky, Navy Capt. William S. Parsons eased himself into the bomb bay to begin the delicate, dangerous work. As deputy director of the laboratory that had developed and built the weapon, "Deak" Parsons knew more about the inner workings of the bomb than almost anyone on earth. The service revolver he carried at his side—borrowed from a military policeman before takeoff—was Parsons's assurance that he would never be taken alive by the Japanese.

In the tight confines of the bomb bay, Parsons squeezed next to the stubby bomb—14 feet long, 5 feet in diameter, weighing 9,700 pounds. Nicknamed "Little Boy," it was expected to generate the energy equivalent of 20,000 tons of TNT. Using conventional tools, Parsons began his nerve-shattering work.

Twenty-five minutes later, he emerged to report that the nuclear device was armed and ready. A special "black box" in the plane's console would monitor the bomb until its detonation. The *Enola Gay* was not alone in the sky on that fateful August evening. Behind Tibbets were two other B-29's of the 509th Composite Group—one bearing equipment to measure the atomic blast, the other carrying photographers to record the moment for history. A number of scientists were also on board the two planes. Three additional B-29's were an hour ahead of the *Enola Gay*, assigned to monitor the weather over the primary and two alternate targets. A seventh "Superfortress" was standing by at Iwo Jima, ready to take over the mission if Tibbets's plane developed trouble en route.

At 0455, just after daybreak, the *Enola Gay* rendezvoused with the two planes trailing behind. With his cockpit tape recorder running, Tibbets made an official announcement to the 11 men on board. "We're carrying the world's first atomic bomb," he said. There was a gasp, then a long whistle. Although his crew had known the general nature of their mission, it was the first time any of them had heard the weapon described in that way.

With the *Enola Gay* leading a loose V formation, the three B-29's banked lazily to the northwest, bound for Japan and their primary target, the city of Hiroshima.

The atomic bomb had been a marvel of scientific achievement whose development involved some of the world's most brilliant minds.

In 1939, concerned about German experiments in the field of atomic energy, Albert Einstein had written to President Roosevelt, urging that the United States undertake a program of scientific exploration aimed at producing "extremely powerful bombs of a new type."

Roosevelt expressed immediate interest. But it was not until December 6, 1941, that substantial funds were authorized for the purpose of developing such a weapon. The following day, America was at war.

The ultrasecret organization charged with unlocking the secrets of the atom bomb was named The Manhattan Project. Brig. Gen. Leslie R. Groves, a 46-year-old West Point engineer, was chosen to lead it. He began recruiting America's top scientists with all the cold resolve of a local draft board determined to fill its monthly quota.

A remote area in the New Mexico desert, near Los Alamos, was selected as the site for the main research laboratory. Renowned nuclear scientists such as J. Robert Oppenheimer, Edward Teller, and Enrico Fermi joined the top-secret project.

It was Fermi who, on December 2, 1942, in a frigid squash court beneath the stands of the University of Chicago's football stadium, conducted the first controlled nuclear chain reaction, a breakthrough essential to the bomb's development.

America's booming wartime industry soon became involved. Throughout the nation, elements that would make up the weapon—including fissionable material—were developed and processed. Only a handful of the estimated 539,000 people who worked on the bomb knew what they were building.

By late 1944 Gen. Groves estimated that the device would be ready for use by August 1945. Since the war with Germany was already winding down—Hitler's defeat all but assured—it was clear that the bomb would have to be used against Japan.

When the Army Air Force was ordered to organize a special unit to deliver the bomb to its target, the 509th Composite Group was born. Loosely attached to the 21st Bomber Command, the 509th was to receive its orders only from the President—through the Secretary of War.

Activated on December 17, 1944, the unit consisted of 225 officers, 1,542 enlisted men, and 15 brand-new B-29's. Col. Tibbets, chosen to command, took the group to a barren desert site at Wendover, Utah, to begin their training.

Operating under rigid security, the 509th's missions were flown according to strict if not unusual rules: Operations took place at exactly 30,000 feet. Only one bomb—weighing 10,000 pounds—was dropped on each flight. Strict emphasis was placed on visual bombing.

As activities at Los Alamos intensified, consideration was given as to the target. With Iwo Jima and the Philippines in American hands, the Japanese home islands were being ravaged by daily raids. Most of Japan's industry had been crippled by the massive air strikes. Her major cities lay in ruins. A raid against Tokyo on March 9, 1945, resulted in a deadly firestorm that killed 85,000 people and leveled 80 percent of the city.

Only a few Japanese cities had been untouched by the bombing. Among these—making them prime candidates for destruction—were Kyoto, Kokura, and Hiroshima. Nagasaki would be added at the last moment.

On May 29, 1945, when the *Cape Victory* docked at Tinian, most of the 509th Composite Group was mixed in with the 21st Bomber Command's June replacements. In her daily radio program, the ever-resourceful Tokyo Rose announced the 509th's arrival.

On August 2nd, Hiroshima was chosen as the primary target. The attack was scheduled for the morning of August 6th. Tibbets and the 509th were placed on full alert. The countdown leading to their historic flight began.

At 7:09 A.M. on August 6th, the B-29 *Straight Flush*, a weather plane with Capt. Claude Eatherly at the controls, passed over Hiroshima. Thirty thousand feet below, an air raid alarm sounded in the city.

Eatherly, normally a flamboyant, hell-raising officer, gloomily considered the thick cover of clouds below him. Since visual bombing had been ordered, it seemed that Hiroshima might be spared. Two other 509th weather planes were already over the alternate targets—Kokura and Nagasaki. Weather conditions at both these sites had already been reported as favorable for a bomb drop.

Capt. Eatherly flew toward Tibbets's aiming point, the T-shaped Aioi Bridge at the city's center. Suddenly, a break in the clouds appeared. Below him, Hiroshima lay open and inviting in the full glare of the morning sun.

Eatherly rolled the *Straight Flush* into a wide turn and made a second pass over the city. The widening break in the clouds was now more than 10 miles across. His radio message to Tibbets doomed Hiroshima. "Advice: bomb primary," it said.

At 0730, the *Enola Gay* flew over the edge of Shikoku Island, bound for Hiroshima. All on board donned flak suits except for tail gunner Bob Caron, jammed into the rear turret. After several attempts to struggle into the bulky jacket, he let his slip to the floor.

Tibbets reminded everyone to lower their protective glasses following the bomb drop. Then, flying at an altitude of 31,600 feet, he began his run to the target.

Hunched over his bombsight, Maj. Thomas W. Ferebee saw his target slide into view. Seconds later, his crosshairs pinpointed

Hiroshima's Aioi Bridge. At precisely 08:15:17, the bomb bay doors snapped open and "Little Boy" careened earthward.

At 08:16:00, Hiroshima disappeared in a blinding light. A fireball, 1,800 feet across and 100 million degrees at the center, consumed most of the city. Ferebee's bomb had landed only 200 yards from its aiming point.

Survivors would later say that the blast looked like a photographer's flash bulb exploding before them. More than 70,000 died instantly, most incinerated where they stood. As many others were horribly burned. Thousands would die within days of radiation sickness. Four square miles of Hiroshima had been erased, 80 percent of its buildings flattened. Doctors, nurses, and firefighters were among the victims. Water mains were destroyed. Fires raged out of control. Thousands of citizens, frantic to escape the holocaust, sought refuge in the river. Most of them died horribly in its boiling waters. Everywhere, the destruction was catastrophic.

Following the bomb drop, Tibbets threw the plane into a violent evasive turn. In the tail, Sgt. Caron watched for the explosion. When it came, there was a deathly silence aboard as the crew watched the giant mushroom cloud rise to a height of 60,000 feet. Later, one would describe the scene as "looking into a vat of boiling oil." Another would call it "a peep into Hell."

Two powerful shock waves shook the *Enola Gay*. There had been fears that the explosion might knock Tibbets out of the sky. But he retained control and banked the plane for another run over the city.

Where Hiroshima had stood moments before—there was nothing. Countless fires raged beneath the boiling cloud that continued to rise above the devastation.

Tibbets's message to Tinian reported that the raid had been a complete success. After a final run over the burning city, he set the *Enola Gay* on a course for home.

On August 9th, the Japanese surrender not forthcoming, a second nuclear device—this one a plutonium bomb—was unleashed on the city of Nagasaki. More powerful than the Alamagordo weapon, it resulted in an additional 100,000 casualties.

Five days later, a stunned Japan capitulated. The formal surrender ceremonies took place on September 2, 1945, aboard the U.S.S. *Missouri*, anchored in Tokyo Bay.

After six years and 55 million lives, World War II, the greatest conflict in human history, was over.

At its end, the world had been thrust into a nuclear age fraught with danger and uncertainty. Man now possessed the power to destroy mankind and nothing would ever be the same. Said Winston Churchill, "I fear the Dark Ages may return on the gleaming wings of science."

India, 1942. One of General Claire Chennault's "Flying Tigers."

Rabaul, January 1944. A Japanese cruiser and transports under attack by U.S. bombers.

Rabaul. A 5th Air Force B-24 of the 345th Bomb Group attacks this Japanese destroyer at masthead height.

Rabaul Harbor. A Japanese heavy cruiser takes a direct hit from U.S. bombers.

A violent explosion on a Japanese destroyer escort hit by U.S. bombers. 1944.

Tinian, Marianas Islands. The *Enola Gay*.

"Little Boy," the atomic bomb dropped on Hiroshima.

The mushroom cloud over Hiroshima. At the time this photograph was made, smoke billowed 20,000 feet above Hiroshima. The smoke from the first atomic bomb spread over 10,000 feet at the base of the rising column. The date: August 6, 1945. Two planes from the 509th Composite Bomb Group, part of the 303rd Wing of the 20th Air Force, participated. One plane dropped "Little Boy," the other B-29 was an escort.

The *Enola Gay* returns to park after the bombing of Hiroshima.

The ground and flight crew of *Enola Gay* after dropping the first atomic bomb on Hiroshima. Paul W. Tibbets, the pilot, is in the center under the prop, wearing a shirt and cap. Tinian, Marianas Islands.

Hiroshima. Concussion at some distance from Ground Zero caused the collapse of this Hiroshima railway bridge.

Hiroshima in 1945. This view from the Red Cross Buildings was taken 1 mile from Ground Zero.

Yokohama, August 30, 1945. The city lies in ruins after repeated bombing by B-29s.

This modern steel structure withstood the firebombing raids on Tokyo. Photograph taken on August 30, 1945.

Yokohama, August 31, 1945. General of the Army Douglas MacArthur greets General Jonathan Wainwright, their first meeting since MacArthur had left Corregidor in 1941. Wainwright had been in a Japanese prison camp for 4 years.

September 2, 1945. The surrender ceremony aboard the battleship USS *Missouri*. Admiral Chester Nimitz signs surrender document.

Mamory Shigemitsu signs the surrender document for Japan.

Washington, D.C., September 7, 1945. Surrender documents arrive at the White House and are presented to President Harry S Truman.

President Franklin Delano Roosevelt at Camp Shelby, Mississippi, visiting GI's in 1942.

Casablanca Conference, January 14, 1943. President Roosevelt confers with his son, Major Elliot Roosevelt, who was serving as his aide.

Lieutenant Generals Courtney Hodges (left), Omar N. Bradley (center), and George S. Patton.

November 26, 1943. Premier Joseph V. Stalin at the Teheran Conference. It was his first meeting with Roosevelt and Churchill.

Castelventrano, Sicily, December 8, 1943.
FDR and General Eisenhower prepare to in-
spect the troops.

The Yalta Conference, February 1945. The
last international conference at which Prime
Minister Winston S. Churchill, President
Franklin Delano Roosevelt, and Premier Joseph V. Stalin would meet. Standing behind
the leaders are Foreign Minister Anthony
Eden, Secretary of State Edward Stettinius,
and Foreign Minister V. M. Molotov.

A photograph of two "Former Naval Per-
sons" at Yalta. FDR's health was failing. He
had less than 4 months to live.

General Dwight D. Eisenhower.

Lieutenant General Simon Bolivar Buckner, commanding general, Central Pacific. He was killed by artillery fire on Okinawa in 1945.